THE
SHEPHERD'S CALENDAR

To Tim, my new co-editor, from

Eric H Robinson

JOHN CLARE

THE SHEPHERD'S
CALENDAR

EDITED BY ERIC ROBINSON AND
GEOFFREY SUMMERFIELD

With wood engravings by David Gentleman

OXFORD UNIVERSITY PRESS

Oxford University Press, Walton Street, Oxford OX2 6DP

Oxford New York Toronto
Delhi Bombay Calcutta Madras Karachi
Petaling Jaya Singapore Hong Kong Tokyo
Nairobi Dar es Salaam Cape Town
Melbourne Auckland

and associated companies in
Berlin Ibadan

Oxford is a trade mark of Oxford University Press

ISBN 0–19–281142–8

This edition
© *Oxford University Press 1964, 1973*

First published 1964 by Oxford University Press
and reprinted in 1965, 1968, 1980
First issued as an Oxford University Press paperback 1973
Reprinted 1974, 1975, 1978, 1980, 1981. 1983, 1987, 1990

Printed in Hong Kong

CONTENTS

INTRODUCTION

THE suggestion that Clare should write 'The Shepherd's Calendar' originated with John Taylor, his publisher, in a letter of 1 August 1823; the volume was advertised in January 1824; Clare received the first proofs in March 1825; the book finally appeared in April 1827, and by 1829 only 400 copies had been sold. For Clare this was a time-table of disappointment and defeat. Frustrated by the delays and indecisions of his publisher, angered by the savage editing of his manuscripts, and ultimately unappreciated by the public, he became very moody and listless. Taylor, however, was more concerned with his own troubles:

The Season has been a very bad one for new Books, & I am afraid the Time has passed away in which Poetry will answer . . . the Shepherds Calendar has had comparatively no Sale . . . I think in future I shall confine my Speculations [i.e. financial speculations] to works of Utility—though for my old Friends I may still occasionally run Risques. . . .

And in the meantime Clare struggled on in an intellectual climate which had become inimical to his kind of poetry, except for the few trivia, not really characteristic of him at his best, which were accepted for publication in the Annuals—the 'Keepsakes', the 'Forget-me-nots', the 'Amulets', and the other Victorian bric-à-brac of the book world.

Yet as we look back on 'The Shepherd's Calendar' today, a hundred years after the poet's death, and upon the other poems that appeared in the same volume, it seems that Clare was then in some ways at his very best, and displaying his greatest strengths. First of all the poems could only have been written by someone who knew village life from the inside and whose touch was certain in subjects that might appear sentimental or eccentric if wrongly handled—the poems are full of a sense of village community, of activities shared, and they are therefore some of the most joyful of Clare's writings.[1] Secondly the observations of nature, particularly of flowers and bird life, are those of the finest naturalist in all English poetry, though Taylor was so unsympathetic to them that he cut out some of the best passages before publishing the poem. It is just here that the modern reader is most likely to disagree with John Taylor's observations:

I have often remarked that your Poetry is much the best when you are not describing common things, and if you would raise your Views generally, & speak of the Appearances of Nature each Month more philosophically (if I may so say) or with more Excitement, you would greatly improve these little poems. . . .

Clare's publisher objected to 'the language of common everyday Description' in Clare's poems. With all

[1] The social and economic historian will be particularly interested in several passages in this poem, such as the description of the Scottish drovers moving southwards with their herds, and the tithesmen marking the stooks with green boughs. See pp. 71 and 76–77.

Taylor's education and refinement, his rich and varied acquaintance with the world of literature, his taste was essentially artificial. Like the reading public for the Victorian annuals, he wanted everything blown up, he wanted significant statement pushed into poetry, and his attitude, despite his radical political sympathies, was a moralizing and condescending one. It is odd to see the publisher of Keats and Lamb, at one time defending Clare against the political censorship imposed on him by the poet's evangelical patron, Lord Radstock, and at another himself exercising moral censorship over 'The Shepherd's Calendar'.

Taylor acknowledged to Clare that he had 'been compelled to cut out a vast many lines'. What has not been realized before is the extent of his 'slashings' (Taylor's own word for it) and the reasons for them, some literary, some not. Every month of 'The Shepherd's Calendar' was lopped with greater or lesser brutality. *July* was totally rejected and Clare submitted an alternative version; *December*, in contrast, was only reduced from 152 lines to 128. In total figures the sequence as a whole was reduced from 3,382 lines (i.e. excluding the second version of *July*) to 1,761 lines (excluding the second version of *July*), and *July* was replaced by a completely new poem. Taylor wrote about the latter: 'Instead of cutting out of the poem on July what is bad, I am obliged to look earnestly to find anything that is good.' We disagree. Taylor's statement is palpably false, and made in a moment of anger. The original *July* is not only better than much of Clare's poetry that Taylor published but also better than the 1827 version, and we have printed both versions in this volume that the reader may judge for himself.

Most of Taylor's excisions are frankly unintelligible to us, unless on the supposition that he found many passages too 'unphilosophical', and too concerned with everyday events. For example, was this his reason for cutting out lines 29–100 from *January*? Those lines with their descriptions of the thresher's early morning rising, the foddering boy 'blowing his fingers as he goes', and the boy watering the stock, who:

> At clanking pump his station takes
> Half hid in mist their breathing makes,

seem to us more vitally evocative of the country scene than anything since Shakespeare's little song on 'Winter', and there are several other omissions of the same kind in *January* alone. On other occasions Taylor seems to have cut out lines because they did not agree with his sense of poetical fitness, as when Clare describes fairies crowding in cupboards 'As thick as mites in rotten cheese', where the Cockney's view of fairies was probably more childish and less child-like than the countryman's. This artificial delicacy of Taylor's sometimes makes him as bad as Lord Radstock, and even causes him to omit from a list of flowers in *May* the lines:

> And smell smocks that from view retires
> Mong rustling leaves and bowing briars

because he disliked the country name for a lecher.
And are the last four lines of *June* omitted because
Taylor disliked philosophizing or because the criti-
cism of the social structure might offend his conserva-
tive customers:

> As proud distinction makes a wider space
> Between the genteel and the vulgar race
> Then must they fade as pride oer custom showers
> Its blighting mildew on her feeble flowers?

In Taylor's version, too, the labourer, 'stript in his
shirt', is not allowed to sit beside the maiden 'in her
unpin[ne]d gown'; no criticism of enclosing farmers
or 'tyrant justice' appears; and the labourers are not
even allowed, in that age of industriousness, to be:

> Glad that the harvests end is nigh
> And weary labour nearly bye.

Thus, as Clare complained on 30 April 1825, about
another editor, though at the same period of his differ-
ences with Taylor: 'Editors are troubled with nice
amendings & if Doctors were as fond of amputation as
they are of altering & correcting the world woud have
nothing but cripples.' The truth is that if some lines
had not been deliberately obliterated in Clare's manu-
scripts we should have an even clearer view of what
he really thought about Taylor, since, from their con-
text, they clearly refer to this matter.

But besides his non-literary emendations, Taylor
made a number of alterations to Clare's text for literary

reasons. He tidied up the grammar and corrected the punctuation, and this despite the fact that he had previously advised him not to bother about the study of grammar:

Keep as you are: your Education has better fitted you for a Poet then all [the] School Learning in the world would be able to do.[1]

Yet Taylor's sense of 'correctness', shared by later editors though they have disowned it, sometimes meant that if the grammar were intractable, it was easier to omit lines altogether. Then there were Taylor's alterations of provincial words. These had always troubled him in Clare's verse, but the poet's independence on the matter had obliged him to compromise in the first volume, *Poems Descriptive of Rural Life and Scenery*, even to the extent of allowing a glossary. In 'The Shepherd's Calendar', he was more ruthless, so that many of the words glossed in this volume, and many others that we have printed just as Clare wrote them, are entirely missing from Taylor's edition. Similarly the names of country games are omitted because they were not familiar to the editor. Yet those words, their spellings, and the unusual grammar are integral to the vivacity and the accuracy of Clare's poetic vision. No wonder that he wrote in his Journal for 12 February 1825: 'Receivd a letter from Van Dyk in which he appears as the Editor of my Poems they chose who they please this time but

[1] Taylor to Clare, 17 May 1820.

my choice comes next & I think I shall feel able to do it myself. . . .'

It is now necessary that we should describe our own editorial procedure. We apologize for not giving a full editorial apparatus in this book, but must explain that this will appear in the full edition of Clare's poems which we are preparing for the Oxford English Texts series. We shall there describe all the manuscripts that have been consulted and what our authority is for every line and word, but we feel that this would be too heavy for a text which while being authoritative is directed to the general reader. The only alterations to Clare's words in this edition are minimal, and, we would submit, quite different in character and quantity from those made by Clare's earlier editors. We have substituted 'where' for 'were' throughout when the sense demanded it, and 'ne'er' for Clare's spelling 'near'. These occur so often and are so liable to cause difficulty to the ordinary reader that we thought that we were justified in making these alterations in this particular text. We have also punctuated 'hell', 'shell', 'Ill' to 'he'll', 'she'll', and 'I'll' for the same reason. At *one* point we have printed 'while' for 'whiele'. If a word is omitted, we have inserted it in square brackets, thus [   ]. There is a glossary at the end of the book, but occasionally, when a word is spelt by Clare in such a way that we feel the reader might stumble, we have glossed it at the foot of the page. Otherwise everything remains exactly as Clare wrote it. This may prove a little difficult at first, but the reader will soon adjust himself to Clare's idiom and lack of punctuation, and will not be much troubled by Clare's spelling if he reads the words aloud.

The manuscripts used are from the collection of the Peterborough Museum Society, a society which deserves every help that lovers of Clare's poetry can give, and to which we ourselves owe a great debt. The relevant manuscripts are Peterborough MSS. 1, 9, 12, 16, 25, 29, 37, 64, and 90, but we must refer to our projected edition of the poems for a description of the detailed use we have made of them. Taylor gives twelve lines in *September* which we have found nowhere in the manuscripts, but they are clearly genuine and we have incorporated them in our text. Anyone wishing to see in greater detail our criticisms of Taylor's editing of 'The Shepherd's Calendar' should consult *The Review of English Studies*, New Series, xiv. 56 (November 1963), pp. 359–69.

Here then is Clare's most ambitious single poem— as he wrote it. It is the truest poem of English country life ever written, it is poetry in the mainstream of the English tradition of nature poetry, and it is poetry that is immediately accessible to the ordinary reader.

1964

JANUARY

A WINTERS DAY

Withering and keen the winter comes
While comfort flyes to close shut rooms
And sees the snow in feathers pass
Winnowing by the window glass
And unfelt tempests howl and beat
Above his head in corner seat
And musing oer the changing scene
Farmers behind the tavern screen
Sit—or wi elbow idly prest
On hob reclines the corners guest

1

Reading the news to mark again
The bankrupt lists or price of grain
Or old moores anual prophecys
That many a theme for talk supplys
Whose almanacks thumbd pages swarm
Wi frost and snow and many a storm
And wisdom gossipd from the stars
Of politics and bloody wars
He shakes his head and still proceeds
Neer doubting once of what he reads
All wonders are wi faith supplyd
Bible at once and weather guide
Puffing the while his red tipt pipe
Dreaming oer troubles nearly ripe
Yet not quite lost in profits way
He'll turn to next years harvest day
And winters leisure to regale
Hopes better times and sips his ale
While labour still pursues his way
And braves the tempest as he may
The thresher first thro darkness deep
Awakes the mornings winter sleep
Scaring the owlet from her prey
Long before she dreams of day
That blinks above head on the snow
Watching the mice that squeaks below
And foddering boys sojourn again
By ryhme[1] hung hedge and frozen plain
Shuffling thro the sinking snows
Blowing his fingers as he goes

[1] = rime.

To where the stock in bellowings hoarse
Call for their meals in dreary close
And print full many a hungry track
Round circling hedge that guards the stack
Wi higgling tug he cuts the hay
And bares the forkfull loads away
And morn and evening daily throws
The little heaps upon the snows
The shepherd too in great coat wrapt
And straw bands round his stockings lapt
Wi plodding dog that sheltering steals
To shun the wind behind his heels
Takes rough and smooth the winter weather
And paces thro the snow together
While in the fields the lonly plough
Enjoys its frozen sabbath now
And horses too pass time away
In leisures hungry holiday
Rubbing and lunging round the yard
Dreaming no doubt of summer sward
As near wi idle pace they draw
To brouze the upheapd cribs of straw
While whining hogs wi hungry roar
Crowd around the kitchen door
Or when their scanty meal is done
Creep in the straw the cold to shun
And old hens scratting all the day
Seeks curnels chance may throw away
Pausing to pick the seed and grain
Then dusting up the chaff again

While in the barn holes hid from view
The cats their patient watch pursue
For birds which want in flocks will draw
From woods and fields to pick the straw
The soodling boy that saunters round
The yard on homward dutys bound
Now fills the troughs for noisy hogs
Oft asking aid from barking dogs
That tuggles at each flopping ear
Of such as scramble on too near
Or circld round wi thirsty stock
That for his swinging labours flock
At clanking pump his station takes
Half hid in mist their breathing makes
Or at the pond before the door
Which every night leaves frozen oer
Wi heavy beetle[1] splinters round
The glossy ice wi jarring sound
While huddling geese as half asleep
Doth round the imprisond water creep
Silent and sad to wait his aid
And soon as ere a hole is made
They din his ears wi pleasures cry
And hiss at all that ventures nigh
Splashing wi jealous joys & vain
Their fill ere it be froze again
And woodstack climbs at maids desire
Throwing down faggots for the fire
Where stealing time he often stands
To warm his half froze tingling hands

[1] See Glossary.

4

The schoolboy still in dithering joys
Pastime in leisure hours employs
And be the weather as it may
Is never at a loss for play
Rolling up giant heaps of snow
As noontide frets its little thaw
Making rude things of various names
Snow men or aught their fancy frames
Till numbd wi cold they quake away
And join at hotter sports to play
Kicking wi many a flying bound
The football oer the frozen ground
Or seeking bright glib ice to play
To sailing slide the hours away
As smooth and quick as shadows run
When clouds in autumn pass the sun
Some hurrying rambles eager take
To skait upon the meadow lake
Scaring the snipe from her retreat
From shelving banks unfrozen seat
Or running brook where icy spars
Which the pale sunlight specks wi stars
Shoots crizzling oer the restless tide
To many a likness petrified
Where fancy often stoops to pore
And turns again to wonder more
The more hen too wi fear opprest
Starts from her reedy shelterd nest
Bustling to get from foes away
And scarcly flies more fast then they

5

Skaiting along wi curving springs
Wi arms spread out like herons wings
They race away for pleasures sake
A hunters speed along the lake
And oft neath trees where ice is thin
Meet narrow scapes from breaking in
Again the robin waxes tame
And ventures pitys crumbs to claim
Picking the trifles off the snow
Which dames on purpose daily throw
And perching on the window sill
Where memory recolecting still
Knows the last winters broken pane
And there he hops and peeps again
The clouds of starnels dailey fly
Blackening thro the evening sky
To whittleseas[1] reed wooded mere
And ozier holts by rivers near
And many a mingld swathy crowd
Rook crow and jackdaw noising loud
Fly too and fro to dreary fen
Dull winters weary flight agen
Flopping on heavy wings away
As soon as morning wakens grey
And when the sun sets round and red
Returns to naked woods to bed
Wood pigeons too in flocks appear
By hunger tamd from timid fear

---

[1] Whittlesea, Cambridgeshire. For a map which clearly indicates the extent of this mere, see H. C. Darby, *The Draining of the Fens*, Cambridge, 1956, p. 230.

They mid the sheep unstartld steal
And share wi them a scanty meal
Picking the green leaves want bestows
Of turnips sprouting thro the snows
The ickles from the cottage eaves
Which cold nights freakish labour leaves
Fret in the sun a partial thaw
Pattring on the pitted snow
But soon as ere hes out of sight
They eke afresh their tails at night
The sun soon creepeth out of sight
Behind the woods—and running night
Makes haste to shut the days dull eye
And grizzles oer the chilly sky
Dark deep and thick by day forsook
As cottage chimneys sooty nook
While maidens fresh as summer roses
Joining from the distant closes
Haste home wi yokes and swinging pail
And thresher too sets by his flail
And leaves the mice at peace agen
To fill their holes wi stolen grain
And owlets glad his toils are oer
Swoops by him as he shuts the door
The shepherd seeks his cottage warm
And tucks his hook beneath his arm
And weary in the cold to roam
Scenting the track that leadeth home
His dog wi swifter pace proceeds
And barks to urge his masters speed

7

Then turns and looks him in the face
And trots before wi mending pace
Till out of whistle from the swain
He sits him down and barks again
Anxious to greet the opend door
And meet the cottage fire once more
The robin that wi nimble eye
Glegs round a danger to espy
Now pops from out the opend door
From crumbs half left upon the floor
Nor wipes his bill on perching chair
Nor stays to clean a feather there
Scard at the cat that sliveth in
A chance from evenings glooms to win
To jump on chairs or tables nigh
Seeking what plunder may supply
The childerns litterd scraps to thieve
Or aught that negligence may leave
Creeping when huswives cease to watch
Or dairey doors are off the latch
On cheese or butter to regale
Or new milk reeking in the pale
The hedger now in leathern coat
From woodland wilds and fields remote
After a journey far and slow
Knocks from his shoes the caking snow
And opes the welcome creaking door
Throwing his faggot on the floor
And at his listening wifes desire
To eke afresh the blazing fire

JANUARY · A WINTERS DAY

Wi sharp bill cuts the hazel bands
Then sets him down to warm his hands
And tell in labours happy way
His story of the passing day
While as the warm blaze cracks and gleams
The supper reeks in savoury steams
Or keetle simmers merrily
And tinkling cups are set for tea
Thus doth the winters dreary day
From morn to evening wear away

JANUARY

A COTTAGE EVENING

The shutter closd the lamp alight
The faggot chopt and blazing bright
The shepherd from his labour free
Dancing his childern on his knee
Or toasting sloe boughs sputtering ripe
Or smoaking glad his puthering pipe
While underneath his masters seat
The tird dog lies in slumbers sweet
Startling and whimpering in his sleep
Chasing still the straying sheep
The cat rolld round in vacant chair
Or leaping childerns knees to lair
Or purring on the warmer hearth
Sweet chorus to the crickets mirth
The redcap hanging over head
In cage of wire is perchd abed
Slumbering in his painted feathers
Unconcious of the outdoor weathers
And things wi out the cottage walls
Meet comfort as the evening falls
As happy in the winters dearth
As those around the blazing hearth

The ass frost drove from off the moors
Where storms thro naked bushes roars
And not a leaf or sprig of green
On ground or quaking bush is seen
Save grey veind ivys hardy pride
Round old trees by the common side
Litterd wi straw now dozes warm
Neath the yard hovel from the storm
The swine well fed and in the sty
And fowl snug perchd in hovel nigh
Wi head in feathers safe asleep
Where fox find ne'er a hole to creep
And geese that gabble in their dreams
Of litterd corn and thawing streams
The sparrow too their daily guest
Is in the cottage eves at rest
And robin small and smaller wren
Are in their warm holes safe agen
From falling snows that winnow bye
The hovels where they nightly lye
And ague winds that shake the tree
Where other birds are forcd to be
The huswife busy night and day
Cleareth the supper things away
While jumping cat starts from her seat
And streaking up on weary feet
The dog wakes at the welcome tones
That calls him up to pick the bones
On corner walls a glittering row
Hang fire irons less for use then show

Tongues bright wi huswifes rubbing toil
Whod sooner burn her hands then soil
When sticks want mending up and when
Mores sought to eke the blaze agen
And sifter[1] dengling by their side
And poker in the fire untryd
And horshoe brightend as a spell
Witchcrafts evil powers to quell
And warming pan reflecting bright
The crackling blazes twittering light
That hangs the corner wall to grace
And seldom taken from its place
Save when the winter keener falls
Searching thro the cottage walls
Then quaking from the cottage fire
Warm beds as comforts they require
Yet still tis bright as gold can be
And childern often peep to see
Their laughing faces as they pass
Gleam on the lid as plain as glass
Things cleard away then down she sits
And tells her tales by starts and fits
Not willing to loose time or toil
She knits or sues[2] and talks the while
Somthing as may be warnings found
To the young listners gaping round
Of boys who in her early day
Strolld to the meadow lake to play
And skaited races void of fear
Oer deeps or shallows any where

[1] See Glossary.   [2] = sews.

12

Till willows oer the brink inclind
Shelterd the water from the wind
And left it scarcly crizzld oer
When one plopt in to rise no more
And how upon a market night
When ne'er a star bestowd its light
A farmers shepherd oer his glass
Forgot that he had woods to pass
Who overtook by darkness deep
Had been to sell his masters sheep
Till coming wi his startld horse
To where two roads a hollow cross
Where lone guide when a stranger strays
A white post points four different ways
There by the woodsides lonly gate
A murdering robber lay in wait
The frighted horse wi broken rein
Stood at the stable door again
But none came home to fill his rack
Or take the saddle from his back
The saddle it was all he bore
The man was seen alive no more
In her young days beside the wood
The gibbet in its terror stood
Tho now all gone tis not forgot
Still dreaded as a haunted spot
And from her memory oft repeats
Witches dread powers and fairey feats
How one has oft been known to prance
In cowcribs like a coach to france

And rid[1] on sheep trays from the fold
A race horse speed to burton hold[2]
To join the midnight mysterys rout
Where witches meet the year about
And how when met wi unawares
They instant turn to cats or hares
And race along wi hellish flight
Now here and there and out of sight
And how the tother tiny things
Will leave their moonlight meadow rings
And unpercievd thro keyholes creep
When alls in bed and fast asleep
And crowd in cupboards as they please
As thick as mites in rotten cheese
To feast on what the cotter leaves
For mice ant[3] reckond bigger thieves
They take away too well as[4] eat
And still the huswifes eye they cheat
Nothing to miss as other thieves
Alls left the same as she percieves
In spite of all the crowds that swarm
In cottage small and larger farm
That thro each key hole pop and pop
Like wasps into a grocers shop
Wi all the things that they can win
From chance to put their plunders in

[1] = rode.
[2] Burton Hold = Burton Old or Burton Wold. See A. Mawer and F. M. Stenton, *The Place Names of Northamptonshire*, 1933, p. 180.
[3] See Glossary.   [4] = as well as.

The shells of wallnuts split in two
By crows who wi the curnels flew
And acorn cups by stock doves pluckt
And eggshells by a cuckoo suckt
That hold what ever things they please
Stole tea or sugar bread or cheese
Wi broad leaves of the sycamore
To rap¹ as cloths their daintys oer
And hazel nutts when they regale
In cellars brought to hold their ale
Wi bungholes squirrels bored well
To get the curnel from the shell
Or maggots a way out to win
When all was eat that grew within
And be the keyholes ere so high
Rush poles a laders help supply
Where soft the climbers fearless tread
On spindles made of benty thread
And foul or fair or dark the night
Their wild fire lamps are ready light
For which full many a daring crime
Is acted in the summer time
When glow worms found in lanes remote
Is murderd for its shining coat
And put in flowers that nature weaves
Wi hollow shapes and silken leaves
Such as the canterbury bell
Serving for lamp or lanthorn well
Or following wi unwearied watch
The flight of one they cannot match

¹ = wrap.

15

As silence sliveth upon sleep
Or thieves by dozing watchdogs creep
They steal from Jack a lanthorns tails
A light whose guidance never fails
To aid them in the darkest night
And guide their plundering steps aright
Rattling away in printless tracks
Some hoisd on beetles glossy backs
Go wisking on and others hie
As fast as loaded moths can flye
Some urge the morning cock to shun
The hardest gallop mice can run
In chariots lolling at their ease
Made of what ere their fancys please
Things that in childhoods memory dwells
Scoopd crow-pot-stones or cockle shells
Wi weels at hand of mallow seeds
Where childish sports were stringing beads
And thus equipd they softly pass
Like shadows on the summer grass
And drive away in troops together
Just as the spring wind drives a feather
They ride oer insects as a stone
Nor bruize a limb nor brake a bone
As light as happy dreams they creep
Nor brake the feeblest link of sleep
A midgeon in their road abed
Neer feels the wheels run oer his head
But sleeps till sunrise calls him up
Unconsous of the passing troop

Thus dames the winter night regales
Wi wonders never ceasing tales
While in the corner ill at ease
Or crushing tween their fathers knees
The childern silent all the while
And een repressd the laugh or smile
Quake wi the ague chills of fear
And tremble while they love to hear
Startling while they the tales recall
At their own shadows on the wall
Till the old clock that strikes unseen
Behind the picture pasted screene
Where Eve and Adam still agree
To rob lifes fatal apple tree
Counts over bed times hour of rest
And bids each be sleep['s] fearful guest
She then her half told tales will leave
To finish on tomorrows eve
The childern cringe away to bed
And up the ladder softly tread
Scarce daring from their fearful joys
To look behind or make a noise
Nor speak a word but still as sleep
They secret to their pillows creep
And whisper oer in terrors way
The prayers they dare no louder say
And hide their heads beneath the cloaths
And try in vain to seek repose
While yet to fancys sleepless eye
Witches on sheep trays gallop bye

And faireys like to rising sparks
Swarm twittering round them in the dark
Till sleep creeps nigh to ease their cares
And drops upon them unawares
O spirit of the days gone bye
Sweet childhoods fearful extacy
The witching spells of winter nights
Where are they fled wi their delights
When listning on the corner seat
The winter evenings length to cheat
I heard my mothers memory tell
Tales superstition loves so well
Things said or sung a thousand times
In simple prose or simpler ryhmes
Ah where is page of poesy
So sweet as theirs was wont to be
The magic wonders that decievd
When fictions were as truths believd
The fairey feats that once prevaild
Told to delight and never faild
Where are they now their fears and sighs
And tears from founts of happy eyes
Breathless suspense and all their crew
To what wild dwelling have they flew
I read in books but find them not
For poesy hath its youth forgot
I hear them told to childern still
But fear ne'er numbs my spirits chill
I still see faces pale wi dread
While mine coud laugh at what is said

See tears imagind woes supply
While mine wi real cares are dry
Where are they gone the joys and fears
The links the life of other years
I thought they bound around my heart
So close that we coud never part
Till reason like a winters day
Nipt childhoods visions all away
Nor left behind one withering flower
To cherish in a lonely hour
Memory may yet the themes repeat
But childhoods heart doth cease to beat
At storys reasons sterner lore
Turneth like gossips from her door
The magic fountain where the head
Rose up just as the startld maid
Was stooping from the weedy brink
To dip her pitcher in to drink
That did its half hid mystery tell
To smooth its hair and use it well
Who doing as it bade her do
Turnd to a king and lover too
The tale of Cinderella told
The winter thro and never old
The faireys favourite and friend
Who made her happy in the end
The pumpkin that at her approach
Was turnd into a golden coach
The rats that faireys magic knew
And instantly to horses grew

And coachmen ready at her call
To drive her to the princes ball
With fur changd jackets silver lind
And tails hung neath their hats behind
Where soon as met the princes sight
She made his heart ach all the night
The golden glove wi fingers small
She lost while dancing in the hall
That was on every finger tryd
And fitted hers and none beside
When cinderella soon as seen
Was woo'd and won and made a queen
The boy that did the jiants slay
And gave his mothers cows away
For magic mask that day or night
When on woud keep him out of sight
And running beans not such as weaves
Round poles the height of cottage eves
But magic ones that travelld high
Some steeples journeys up the sky
And reachd a jiants dwelling there
A cloud built castle in the air
Where venturing up the fearfull height
That servd him climbing half the night
He searchd the jiants coffers oer
And never wanted wealth no more
While like a lion scenting food
The jiant roard in hungry mood
A storm of threats that might suffice
To freeze the hottest blood to ice

And make when heard however bold
The strongest heart strings cramp wi cold
But mine sleeps on thro fear and dread
And terrors that might wake the dead
When like a tiger in the wood
He snufts and tracks the scent of blood
And vows if aught falls in his power
He'll grind their very bones to flower[1]
I hear it now nor dream of harm
The storm is settld to a calm
Those fears are dead what will not dye
In fading lifes mortality
Those truths are fled and left behind
A real world and doubting mind

[1] = flour.

FEBRUARY

A THAW

The snow is gone from cottage tops
The thatch moss glows in brighter green
And eves in quick succession drops
Where grinning icles once hath been
Pit patting wi a pleasant noise
In tubs set by the cottage door
And ducks and geese wi happy joys
Douse in the yard pond brimming oer

The sun peeps thro the window pane
Which childern mark wi laughing eye
And in the wet street steal again
To tell each other spring is nigh
And as young hope the past recalls
In playing groups will often draw
Building beside the sunny walls
Their spring-play-huts of sticks or straw

And oft in pleasures dreams they hie
Round homsteads by the village side
Scratting the hedgrow mosses bye
Where painted pooty shells abide
Mistaking oft the ivy spray
For leaves that come wi budding spring
And wondering in their search for play
Why birds delay to build and sing

The milkmaid singing leaves her bed
As glad as happy thoughts can be
While magpies chatter oer her head
As jocund in the change as she
Her cows around the closes stray
Nor lingering wait the foddering boy
Tossing the molehills in their play
And staring round in frolic joy

Ploughmen go whistling to their toils
And yoke again the rested plough
And mingling oer the mellow soils
Boys' shouts and whips are noising now

The shepherd now is often seen
By warm banks oer his work to bend
Or oer a gate or stile to lean
Chattering to a passing friend

Odd hive bees fancying winter oer
And dreaming in their combs of spring
Creeps on the slab beside their door
And strokes its legs upon its wing
While wild ones half asleep are humming
Round snowdrop bells a feeble note
And pigions coo of summer coming
Picking their feathers on the cote

The barking dogs by lane and wood
Drive sheep afield from foddering ground
And eccho in her summer mood
Briskly mocks the cheery sound
The flocks as from a prison broke
Shake their wet fleeces in the sun
While following fast a misty smoke
Reeks from the moist grass as they run

Nor more behind his masters heels
The dog creeps oer his winter pace
But cocks his tail and oer the fields
Runs many a wild and random chase
Following in spite of chiding calls
The startld cat wi harmless glee
Scaring her up the weed green walls
Or mossy mottld apple tree

As crows from morning perches flye
He barks and follows them in vain
Een larks will catch his nimble eye
And off he starts and barks again
Wi breathless haste and blinded guess
Oft following where the hare hath gone
Forgetting in his joys excess
His frolic puppy days are done

The gossips saunter in the sun
As at the spring from door to door
Of matters in the village done
And secret newsings mutterd oer
Young girls when they each other meet
Will stand their tales of love to tell
While going on errands down the street
Or fetching water from the well

A calm of pleasure listens round
And almost whispers winter bye
While fancy dreams of summer sounds
And quiet rapture fills the eye
The sun beams on the hedges lye
The south wind murmurs summer soft
And maids hang out white cloaths to dry
Around the eldern skirted croft

Each barns green thatch reeks in the sun
Its mate the happy sparrow calls
And as nest building spring begun
Peeps in the holes about the walls

The wren a¹ sunny side the stack
Wi short tail ever on the strunt
Cockd gadding up above his back
Again for dancing gnats will hunt

The gladdend swine bolt from the sty
And round the yard in freedom run
Or stretching in their slumbers lye
Beside the cottage in the sun
The young horse whinneys to its mate
And sickens from the threshers door
Rubbing the straw yards banded gate
Longing for freedom on the moor

Hens leave their roosts wi cackling calls
To see the barn door free from snow
And cocks flye up the mossy walls
To clap their spangld wings and crow
About the steeples sunny top
The jackdaw flocks resemble spring
And in the stone archd windows pop
Wi summer noise and wanton wing

The small birds think their wants are oer
To see the snow hills fret again
And from the barns chaff litterd door
Betake them to the greening plain
The woodmans robin startles coy
Nor longer at his elbow comes
To peck wi hungers eager joy
Mong mossy stulps the litterd crumbs

¹ See Glossary.

Neath hedge and walls that screen the wind
The gnats for play will flock together
And een poor flyes odd hopes will find
To venture in the mocking weather
From out their hiding holes again
Wi feeble pace they often creep
Along the sun warmd window pane
Like dreaming things that walk in sleep

The mavis thrush wi wild delight
Upon the orchards dripping tree
Mutters to see the day so bright
Spring scraps of young hopes poesy
And oft dame stops her burring wheel
To hear the robins note once more
That tutles while he pecks his meal
From sweet briar hips beside the door

The hedghog from its hollow root
Sees the wood moss clear of snow
And hunts each hedge for fallen fruit
Crab hip and winter bitten sloe
And oft when checkd by sudden fears
As shepherd dog his haunt espies
He rolls up in a ball of spears
And all his barking rage defies

Thus nature of the spring will dream
While south winds thaw but soon again
Frost breaths upon the stiffening stream
And numbs it into ice—the plain

Soon wears its merry garb of white
And icicles that fret at noon
Will eke their icy tails at night
Beneath the chilly stars and moon

Nature soon sickens of her joys
And all is sad and dumb again
Save merry shouts of sliding boys
About the frozen furrowd plain
The foddering boy forgets his song
And silent goes wi folded arms
And croodling shepherds bend along
Crouching to the whizzing storms

MARCH

March month of 'many weathers' wildly comes
In hail and snow and rain and threatning hums
And floods: while often at his cottage door
The shepherd stands to hear the distant roar
Loosd from the rushing mills and river locks
Wi thundering sound and over powering shocks
And headlong hurry thro the meadow brigs
Brushing the leaning sallows fingering twigs
In feathery foam and eddy hissing chase
Rolling a storm oertaken travellers pace
From bank to bank along the meadow leas
Spreading and shining like to little seas

While in the pale sunlight a watery brood
Of swopping white birds flock about the flood
Yet winter seems half weary of its toil
And round the ploughman on the elting soil
Will thread a minutes sunshine wild and warm
Thro the raggd places of the swimming storm
And oft the shepherd in his path will spye
The little daisey in the wet grass lye
That to the peeping sun enlivens gay
Like Labour smiling on an holiday
And where the stunt bank fronts the southern sky
By lanes or brooks where sunbeams love to lye
A cowslip peep will open faintly coy
Soon seen and gatherd by a wandering boy
A tale of spring around the distant haze
Seems muttering pleasures wi the lengthening days
Morn wakens mottld oft wi may day stains
And shower drops hang the grassy sprouting plains
And on the naked thorns of brassy hue
Drip glistning like a summer dream of dew
While from the hill side freshing forest drops
As one might walk upon their thickening tops
And buds wi young hopes promise seemly swells
Where woodman that in wild seclusion dwells
Wi chopping toil the coming spring decieves
Of many dancing shadows flowers and leaves
And in his pathway down the mossy wood
Crushes wi hasty feet full many a bud
Of early primrose yet if timely spied
Shelterd some old half rotten stump beside

MARCH

The sight will cheer his solitery hour
And urge his feet to stride and save the flower
Muffld in baffles leathern coat and gloves
The hedger toils oft scaring rustling doves
From out the hedgrows who in hunger browze
The chockolate berrys on the ivy boughs
And flocking field fares speckld like the thrush
Picking the red awe from the sweeing bush
That come and go on winters chilling wing
And seem to share no sympathy wi spring
The stooping ditcher in the water stands
Letting the furrowd lakes from off the lands
Or splashing cleans the pasture brooks of mud
Where many a wild weed freshens into bud
And sprouting from the bottom purply green
The water cresses neath the wave is seen
Which the old woman gladly drags to land
Wi reaching long rake in her tottering hand
The ploughman mawls along the doughy sloughs
And often stop their songs to clean their ploughs
From teazing twitch that in the spongy soil
Clings round the colter terryfying toil
The sower striding oer his dirty way
Sinks anckle deep in pudgy sloughs and clay
And oer his heavy hopper stoutly leans
Strewing wi swinging arms the pattering beans
Which soon as aprils milder weather gleams
Will shoot up green between the furroed seams
The driving boy glad when his steps can trace
The swelling edding as a resting place

31

Slings from his clotted shoes the dirt around
And feign[1] woud rest him on the solid ground
And sings when he can meet the parting green
Of rushy balks that bend the lands between
While close behind em struts the nauntling crow
And daws whose heads seem powderd oer wi snow
To seek the worms—and rooks a noisey guest
That on the wind rockd elms prepares her nest
On the fresh furrow often drops to pull
The twitching roots and gathering sticks and wool
Neath trees whose dead twigs litter to the wind
And gaps where stray sheep left their coats behind
While ground larks on a sweeing clump of rushes
Or on the top twigs of the oddling bushes
Chirp their 'cree creeing' note that sounds of spring
And sky larks meet the sun wi flittering wing
Soon as the morning opes its brightning eye
Large clouds of sturnels blacken thro the sky
From oizer holts about the rushy fen
And reedshaw borders by the river Nen
And wild geese regiments now agen repair
To the wet bosom of broad marshes there
In marching coloms and attention all
Listning and following their ringleaders call
The shepherd boy that hastens now and then
From hail and snow beneath his sheltering den
Of flags or file leavd sedges tyd in sheaves
Or stubble shocks oft as his eye percieves
Sun threads struck out wi momentery smiles
Wi fancy thoughts his lonliness beguiles

[1] = fain.

MARCH

Thinking the struggling winter hourly bye
As down the edges of the distant sky
The hailstorm sweeps—and while he stops to strip
The stooping hedgbriar of its lingering hip
He hears the wild geese gabble oer his head
And pleasd wi fancys in his musings bred
He marks the figurd forms in which they flye
And pausing follows wi a wandering eye
Likening their curious march in curves or rows
To every letter which his memory knows
While far above the solitary crane
Swings lonly to unfrozen dykes again
Cranking a jarring mellancholy cry
Thro the wild journey of the cheerless sky
Full oft at early seasons mild and fair
March bids farewell wi garlands in her hair
Of hazzel tassles woodbines hairy sprout
And sloe and wild plumb blossoms peeping out
In thickset knotts of flowers preparing gay
For aprils reign a mockery of may
That soon will glisten on the earnest eye
Like snow white cloaths hung in the sun to drye
The old dame often stills her burring wheel
When the bright sun will thro the window steal
And gleam upon her face and dancing fall
In diamond shadows on the picturd wall
While the white butterflye as in amaze
Will settle on the glossy glass to gaze
And oddling bee oft patting passing bye
As if they care to tell her spring was nigh

And smiling glad to see such things once more
Up she will get and potter to the door
And look upon the trees beneath the eves
Sweet briar and ladslove swelling into leaves
And damsin trees thick notting into bloom
And goosberry blossoms on the bushes come
And stooping down oft views her garden beds
To see the spring flowers pricking out their heads
And from her apron strings she'll often pull
Her sissars out an early bunch to cull
For flower pots on the window board to stand
Where the old hour glass spins its thread of sand
And maids will often mark wi laughing cye
In elder where they hang their cloaths to drye
The sharp eyd robin hop from grain to grain
Singing its little summer notes again
As a sweet pledge of Spring the little lambs
Bleat in the varied weather round their dams
Or hugh molehill or roman mound behind
Like spots of snow lye shelterd from the wind
While the old yoes bold wi paternal cares
Looses their fears and every danger dares
Who if the shepherds dog but turns his eye
And stops behind a moment passing bye
Will stamp draw back and then their threats repeat
Urging defiance wi their stamping feet
And stung wi cares hopes cannot recconsile
They stamp and follow till he leaps a stile
Or skulking from their threats betakes to flight
And wi the master lessens out of sight

MARCH

Clowns mark the threatning rage of march pass bye
And clouds wear thin and ragged in the sky
While wi less sudden and more lasting smiles
The growing sun their hopes of spring beguiles
Who often at its end remark wi pride
Days lengthen in their visits a 'cocks stride'
Dames clean their candlesticks and set them bye
Glad of the makeshift light that eves supply
The boy returning home at night from toil
Down lane and close oer footbrig gate and style[1]
Oft trembles into fear and stands to hark
The waking fox renew his short gruff bark
While badgers eccho their dread evening shrieks
And to his thrilling thoughts in terror speaks
And shepherds that wi in their hulks remain
Night after night upon the chilly plain
To watch the dropping lambs that at all hours
Come in the quaking blast like early flowers
Demanding all the shepherds care who find
Warm hedge side spots and take them from the wind
And round their necks in wary caution tyes
Long shreds of rags in red or purple dyes
Thats meant in danger as a safty spell
Like the old yoe that wears a tinkling bell
The sneaking foxes from his thefts to fright
That often seizes the young lambs at night
These when they in their nightly watchings hear
The badgers shrieks can hardly stifle fear
They list the noise from woodlands dark recess
Like helpless shrieking woman in distress

[1] = stile.

35

And oft as such fears fancying mystery
Believes the dismal yelling sounds to be
For superstition hath its thousand tales
To people all his midnight woods and vales
And the dread spot from whence the dismal noise
Mars the night musings of their dark employs
Owns its sad tale to realize their fear
At which their hearts in boyhood achd to hear
A maid at night by treacherous love decoyd
Was in that shrieking wood years past destroyd
She went twas said to meet the waiting swain
And home and friends ne'er saw her face again
Mid brakes and thorns that crowded round the dell
And matting weeds that had no tongues to tell
He murderd her alone at dead midnight
While the pale moon threw round her sickly light
And loud shrieks left the thickets slumbers deep
That only scard the little birds from sleep
When the pale murderers terror frowning eye
Told its dread errand that the maid shoud dye
Mid thick black thorns her secret grave was made
And there ere night the murderd girl was laid
When no one saw the deed but god and he
And moonlight sparkling thro the sleeping tree
Around—the red breast might at morning steel
There for the worm to meet his morning meal
In fresh turnd moulds that first beheld the sun
Nor knew the deed that dismal night had done
Such is the tale that superstition gives
And in her midnight memory ever lives

That makes the boy run by wi wild affright
And shepherds startle on their rounds at night

Now love teazd maidens from their droning wheels
At the red hour of sunset sliving steals
From scolding dames to meet their swains agen
Tho water checks their visits oer the plain
They slive where no one sees some wall behind
Or orchard apple trees that stops the wind
To talk about springs pleasures hoveing nigh
And happy rambles when the roads get dry
The insect world now sunbeams higher climb
Oft dream of spring and wake before their time
Blue flyes from straw stacks crawling scarce alive
And bees peep out on slabs before the hive
Stroaking their little legs across their wings
And venturing short flight where the snow drop
        hings
Its silver bell—and winter aconite
Wi buttercup like flowers that shut at night
And green leaf frilling round their cups of gold
Like tender maiden muffld from the cold
They sip and find their honey dreams are vain
And feebly hasten to their hives again
And butterflys by eager hopes undone
Glad as a child come out to greet the sun
Lost neath the shadow of a sudden shower
Nor left to see tomorrows april flower

APRIL

The infant april joins the spring
And views its watery skye
As youngling linnet trys its wing
And fears at first to flye
With timid step she ventures on
And hardly dares to smile
The blossoms open one by one
And sunny hours beguile

But finer days approacheth yet
With scenes more sweet to charm
And suns arrive that rise and set
Bright strangers to a storm

APRIL

And as the birds with louder song
Each mornings glory cheers
With bolder step she speeds along
And looses all her fears

In wanton gambols like a child
She tends her early toils
And seeks the buds along the wild
That blossom while she smiles
And laughing on with nought to chide
She races with the hours
Or sports by natures lovley side
And fills her lap with flowers

Tho at her birth north cutting gales
Her beautys oft disguise
And hopfull blossoms turning pales[1]
Upon her bosom dies
Yet ere she seeks another place
And ends her reign in this
She leaves us with as fair a face
As ere gave birth to bliss

And fairey month of waking mirth
From whom our joys ensue
Thou early gladder of the earth
Thrice welcom here anew
With thee the bud unfolds to leaves
The grass greens on the lea
And flowers their tender boon recieves
To bloom and smile with thee

[1] Clare seems to have been obsessed by the rhyme here.

APRIL

The shepherds on thy pasture walks
The first fair cowslip finds
Whose tufted flowers on slender stalks
Keep nodding to the winds
And tho thy thorns withold the may
Their shades the violets bring
Which childern stoop for in their play
As tokens of the spring

The time when daiseys bloom divine
With thy calm hours begun
And crowflowers blazing blooms are thine
Bright childern of the sun
Along thy woodlands shaded nooks
The primrose wanly comes
And shining in thy pebley brooks
The horse bleb gaily blooms

The long lost charm of sparkling dew
Thy gentle birth recieves
And on thy wreathing locks we view
The first infolding leaves
And seeking firstling buds and flowers
The trials of thy skill
Were pastimes of my infant hours
And so they haunt me still

To see thy first broad arum leaves
I lovd them from a child
And where thy woodbines sprouting weaves
I joyd to trace the wild

APRIL

And jocund as thy lambs at play
I met the wanton wind
With feelings that have passd away
Whose shadows cling behind

Those joys which childhood claims its own
Woud they were kin to men
Those treasures to the world unknown
When known—was witherd then
But hovering round our growing years
To gild cares sable shroud
Their spirit thro the gloom appears
As suns behind a cloud

As thou first met my infant eyes
When thro thy fields I flew
Whose distance where they meet the skyes
Was all the worlds I knew
That warmth of fancys wildest hours
Which made things kin to life
That heard a voice in trees and flowers
Has swoond in reasons strife

Sweet month thy pleasures bids thee be
The fairest child of spring
And every hour that comes with thee
Comes some new joy to bring
The trees still deepen in their bloom
Grass greens the meadow lands
And flowers with every morning come
As dropt by fairey hands

APRIL

The field and gardens lovley hours
Begin and end with thee
For whats so sweet as peeping flowers
And bursting buds to see
What time the dews unsullied drops
In burnishd gold distills
On crocus flowers unclosing tops
And drooping daffodills

Each day with added glorys come
And as they leave the night
Put on the roseys lovley bloom
And blushes with delight
And suns that wait their welcome birth
With earlier haste pursue
Their journeys to this lower earth
To free their steps from dew

To see thee come all hearts rejoice
And warms with feelings strong
With thee all nature finds a voice
And hums a waking song
The lover views thy welcome hours
And thinks of summer come
And takes the maid thy early flowers
To tempt her steps from home

Along each hedge and sprouting bush
The singing birds are blest
And linnet green and speckld thrush
Prepare their mossy nest

APRIL

On the warm bed thy plain supplys
The young lambs find repose
And mid thy green hills basking lies
Like spots of lingering snows

Young things of tender life again
Enjoys thy sunny hours
And gosslings waddle oer the plain
As yellow as its flowers
Or swim the pond in wild delight
To catch the water flye
Where hissing geese in ceasless spite
Make childern scamper bye

Again the fairey tribes pursue
Their pleasures on the plain
And brightend with the morning dew
Black circles shine again
And on its superstitious ground
Where flowers seem loath to dwell
The toadstools fuzzy balls abound
And mushrooms yearly swell

The seasons beautys all are thine
That visit with the year
Beautys that poets think divine
And all delight to hear
Thy latter days a pleasure brings
That gladden every heart
Pleasures that come like lovley things
But like to shades depart

Thy opend leaves and ripend buds
The cuckoo makes his choice
And shepherds in thy greening woods
First hears the cheering voice
And to thy ripend blooming bowers
The nightingale belongs
And singing to thy parting hours
Keeps night awake with songs

With thee the swallow dares to come
And primes his sutty wings
And urgd to seek their yearly home
Thy suns the Martin brings
And lovley month be leisure mine
Thy yearly mate to be
Tho may day scenes may brighter shine
Their birth belongs to thee

I waked me with thy rising sun
And thy first glorys viewd
And as thy welcome hours begun
Their sunny steps pursued
And now thy sun is on the set
Like to a lovley eve
I view thy parting with regret
And linger loath to leave

Thou lovley april fare thee well
Thou early child of spring
Tho born where storms too often dwell
Thy parents news to bring

APRIL

Yet what thy parting youth supplys
No other months excell
Thou first for flowers and sunny skyes
Sweet april fare thee well

MAY

Come queen of months in company
Wi all thy merry minstrelsy
The restless cuckoo absent long
And twittering swallows chimney song
And hedge row crickets notes that run
From every bank that fronts the sun
And swathy bees about the grass
That stops wi every bloom they pass
And every minute every hour
Keep teazing weeds that wear a flower
And toil and childhoods humming joys
For there is music in the noise

MAY

The village childern mad for sport
In school times leisure ever short
That crick and catch the bouncing ball
And run along the church yard wall
Capt wi rude figured slabs whose claims
In times bad memory hath no names
Oft racing round the nookey church
Or calling ecchos in the porch
And jilting oer the weather cock
Viewing wi jealous eyes the clock
Oft leaping grave stones leaning hights
Uncheckt wi mellancholy sights
The green grass swelld in many a heap
Where kin and friends and parents sleep
Unthinking in their jovial cry
That time shall come when they shall lye
As lowly and as still as they
While other boys above them play
Heedless as they do now to know
The unconcious dust that lies below
The shepherd goes wi happy stride
Wi morns long shadow by his side
Down the dryd lanes neath blooming may
That once was over shoes in clay
While martins twitter neath his eves
Which he at early morning leaves
The driving boy beside his team
Will oer the may month beauty dream
And cock his hat and turn his eye
On flower and tree and deepning skye

And oft bursts loud in fits of song
And whistles as he reels along
Crack[ing] his whip in starts of joy
A happy dirty driving boy
The youth who leaves his corner stool
Betimes for neighbouring village school
While as a mark to urge him right
The church spires all the way in sight
Wi cheerings from his parents given
Starts neath the joyous smiles of heaven
And sawns wi many an idle stand
Wi bookbag swinging in his hand
And gazes as he passes bye
On every thing that meets his eye
Young lambs seem tempting him to play
Dancing and bleating in his way
Wi trembling tails and pointed ears
They follow him and loose their fears
He smiles upon their sunny faces
And feign woud join their happy races
The birds that sing on bush and tree
Seem chirping for his company
And all in fancys idle whim
Seem keeping holiday but him
He lolls upon each resting stile
To see the fields so sweetly smile
To see the wheat grow green and long
And list the weeders toiling song
Or short not[e] of the changing thrush
Above him in the white thorn bush

MAY

That oer the leaning stile bends low
Loaded wi mockery of snow
Mozzld wi many a lushing thread
Of crab tree blossoms delicate red
He often bends wi many a wish
Oer the brig rail to view the fish
Go sturting by in sunny gleams
And chucks in the eye dazzld streams
Crumbs from his pocket oft to watch
The swarming struttle come to catch
Them where they to the bottom sile
Sighing in fancys joy the while
Hes cautiond not to stand so nigh
By rosey milkmaid tripping bye
Where he admires wi fond delight
And longs to be there mute till night
He often ventures thro the day
At truant now and then to play
Rambling about the field and plain
Seeking larks nests in the grain
And picking flowers and boughs of may
To hurd awhile and throw away
Lurking neath bushes from the sight
Of tell tale eyes till schools noon night[1]
Listing each hour for church clocks hum
To know the hour to wander home
That parents may not think him long
Nor dream of his rude doing wrong
Dreading thro the night wi dreaming pain
To meet his masters wand again

[1] i.e. when school ends (night) at noon.

Each hedge is loaded thick wi green
And where the hedger late hath been
Tender shoots begin to grow
From the mossy stumps below
While sheep and cow that teaze the grain
Will nip them to the root again
They lay their bill and mittens bye
And on to other labours hie
While wood men still on spring intrudes
And thins the shadow[s'] solitudes
Wi sharpend axes felling down
The oak trees budding into brown
Where as they crash upon the ground
A crowd of labourers gather round
And mix among the shadows dark
To rip the crackling staining bark
From off the tree and lay when done
The rolls in lares to meet the sun
Depriving yearly where they come
The green wood pecker of its home
That early in the spring began
Far from the sight of troubling man
And bord their round holes in each tree
In fancys sweet security
Till startld wi the woodmans noise
It wakes from all its dreaming joys
The blue bells too that thickly bloom
Where man was never feared to come
And smell smocks that from view retires
Mong rustling leaves and bowing briars

And stooping lilys of the valley
That comes wi shades and dews to dally
White beady drops on slender threads
Wi broad hood leaves above their heads
Like white robd maids in summer hours
Neath umberellas shunning showers
These neath the barkmens crushing treads
Oft perish in their blooming beds
Thus stript of boughs and bark in white
Their trunks shine in the mellow light
Beneath the green surviving trees
That wave above them in the breeze
And waking whispers slowly bends
As if they mournd their fallen friends
Each morning now the weeders meet
To cut the thistle from the wheat
And ruin in the sunny hours
Full many wild weeds of their flowers
Corn poppys that in crimson dwell
Calld 'head achs' from their sickly smell
And carlock yellow as the sun
That oer the may fields thickly run
And 'iron weed' content to share
The meanest spot that spring can spare
Een roads where danger hourly comes
Is not wi out its purple blooms
And leaves wi points like thistles round
Thickset that have no strength to wound
That shrink to childhoods eager hold
Like hair—and with its eye of gold

And scarlet starry points of flowers
Pimpernel dreading nights and showers
Oft calld 'the shepherds weather glass'
That sleep till suns have dyd the grass
Then wakes and spreads its creeping bloom
Till clouds or threatning shadows come
Then close it shuts to sleep again
Which weeders see and talk of rain
And boys that mark them shut so soon
Will call them 'John go bed at noon'
And fumitory too a name
That superstition holds to fame
Whose red and purple mottled flowers
Are cropt by maids in weeding hours
To boil in water milk and way[1]
For washes on an holiday
To make their beauty fair and sleak
And scour the tan from summers cheek
And simple small forget me not
Eyd wi a pinshead yellow spot
I'th'[2] middle of its tender blue
That gains from poets notice due
These flowers the toil by crowds destroys
And robs them of their lowly joys
That met the may wi hopes as sweet
As those her suns in gardens meet
And oft the dame will feel inclind
As childhoods memory comes to mind
To turn her hook away and spare
The blooms it lovd to gather there

[1] = whey.   [2] = In the.

MAY

My wild field catalogue of flowers
Grows in my ryhmes as thick as showers
Tedious and long as they may be
To some, they never weary me
The wood and mead and field of grain
I coud hunt oer and oer again
And talk to every blossom wild
Fond as a parent to a child
And cull them in my childish joy
By swarms and swarms and never cloy
When their lank shades oer morning pearls
Shrink from their lengths to little girls
And like the clock hand pointing one
Is turnd and tells the morning gone
They leave their toils for dinners hour
Beneath some hedges bramble bower
And season sweet their savory meals
Wi joke and tale and merry peals
Of ancient tunes from happy tongues
While linnets join their fitful songs
Perchd oer their heads in frolic play
Among the tufts of motling may
The young girls whisper things of love
And from the old dames hearing move
Oft making 'love knotts' in the shade
Of blue green oat or wheaten blade
And trying simple charms and spells
That rural superstition tells
They pull the little blossom threads
From out the knapweeds button heads

And put the husk wi many a smile
In their white bosoms for awhile
Who if they guess aright the swain
That loves sweet fancys trys to gain
Tis said that ere its lain an hour
Twill blossom wi a second flower
And from her white breasts hankerchief
Bloom as they ne'er had lost a leaf
When signs appear that token wet
As they are neath the bushes met
The girls are glad wi hopes of play
And harping of the holiday
A hugh blue bird will often swim
Along the wheat when skys grow dim
Wi clouds—slow as the gales of spring
In motion wi dark shadowd wing
Beneath the coming storm it sails
And lonly chirps the wheat hid quails
That came to live wi spring again
And start when summer browns the grain
They start the young girls joys afloat
Wi 'wet my foot' its yearly note
So fancy doth the sound explain
And proves it oft a sign of rain
About the moor 'mong sheep and cow
The boy or old man wanders now
Hunting all day wi hopful pace
Each thick sown rushy thistly place
For plover eggs while oer them flye
The fearful birds wi teazing cry

MAY

Trying to lead their steps astray
And coying him another way
And be the weather chill or warm
Wi brown hats truckd beneath his arm
Holding each prize their search has won
They plod bare headed to the sun
Now dames oft bustle from their wheels
Wi childern scampering at their heels
To watch the bees that hang and swive
In clumps about each thronging hive
And flit and thicken in the light
While the old dame enjoys the sight
And raps the while their warming pans
A spell that superstition plans
To coax them in the garden bounds
As if they lovd the tinkling sounds
And oft one hears the dinning noise
Which dames believe each swarm decoys
Around each village day by day
Mingling in the warmth of may
Sweet scented herbs her skill contrives
To rub the bramble platted hives
Fennels thread leaves and crimpld balm
To scent the new house of the swarm
The thresher dull as winter days
And lost to all that spring displays
Still mid his barn dust forcd to stand
Swings his flail round wi weary hand
While oer his head shades thickly creep
And hides the blinking owl asleep

And bats in cobweb corners bred
Sharing till night their murky bed
The sunshine trickles on the floor
Thro every crevice of the door
And makes his barn where shadows dwell
As irksome as a prisoners cell
And as he seeks his daily meal
As schoolboys from their tasks will steal
He often stands in fond delay
To see the daisy in his way
And wild weeds flowering on the wall
That will his childish sports recall
Of all the joys that came wi spring
The twirling top the marble ring
The gingling halfpence hussld up
At pitch and toss the eager stoop
To pick up heads, the smuggeld plays
Neath hovels upon sabbath days
When parson he is safe from view
And clerk sings amen in his pew
The sitting down when school was oer
Upon the threshold by his door
Picking from mallows sport to please
Each crumpld seed he calld a cheese
And hunting from the stackyard sod
The stinking hen banes belted pod
By youths vain fancys sweetly fed
Christning them his loaves of bread
He sees while rocking down the street
Wi weary hands and crimpling feet

MAY

Young childern at the self same games
And hears the self same simple names
Still floating on each happy tongue
Touchd wi the simple scene so strong
Tears almost start and many a sigh
Regrets the happiness gone bye
And in sweet natures holiday
His heart is sad while all is gay
How lovly now are lanes and balks
For toils and lovers sunday walks
The daisey and the buttercup
For which the laughing childern stoop
A hundred times throughout the day
In their rude ramping summer play
So thickly now the pasture crowds
In gold and silver sheeted clouds
As if the drops in april showers
Had woo'd the sun and swoond to flowers
The brook resumes its summer dresses
Purling neath grass and water cresses
And mint and flag leaf swording high
Their blooms to the unheeding eye
And taper bowbent hanging rushes
And horse tail childerns bottle brushes
And summer tracks about its brink
Is fresh again where cattle drink
And on its sunny bank the swain
Stretches his idle length again
Soon as the sun forgets the day
The moon looks down on the lovly may

And the little star his friend and guide
Travelling together side by side
And the seven stars and charleses wain[1]
Hangs smiling oer green woods agen
The heaven rekindles all alive
Wi light the may bees round the hive
Swarm not so thick in mornings eye
As stars do in the evening skye
All all are nestling in their joys
The flowers and birds and pasture boys
The firetail, long a stranger, comes
To his last summer haunts and homes
To hollow tree and crevisd wall
And in the grass the rails odd call
That featherd spirit stops the swain
To listen to his note again
And school boy still in vain retraces
The secrets of his hiding places
In the black thorns crowded cops[e]
Thro its varied turns and stops
The nightingale its ditty weaves
Hid in a multitude of leaves
The boy stops short to hear the strain
And 'sweet jug jug' he mocks again
The yellow hammer builds its nest
By banks where sun beams earliest rest
That drys the dews from off the grass
Shading it from all that pass
Save the rude boy wi ferret gaze
That hunts thro evry secret maze

[1] Charles's Wain = The Plough.

He finds its pencild eggs agen
All streakd wi lines as if a pen
By natures freakish hand was took
To scrawl them over like a book
And from these many mozzling marks
The school boy names them 'writing larks'
Bum barrels twit on bush and tree
Scarse bigger then a bumble bee
And in a white thorns leafy rest
It builds its curious pudding-nest
Wi hole beside as if a mouse
Had built the little barrel house
Toiling full many a lining feather
And bits of grey tree moss together
Amid the noisey rooky park
Beneath the firdales branches dark
The little golden crested wren
Hangs up his glowing nest agen
And sticks it to the furry leaves
As martins theirs beneath the eaves
The old hens leave the roost betimes
And oer the garden pailing climbs
To scrat the gardens fresh turnd soil
And if unwatchd his crops to spoil
Oft cackling from the prison yard
To peck about the houseclose sward
Catching at butterflys and things
Ere they have time to try their wings
The cattle feels the breath of may
And kick and toss their heads in play

The ass beneath his bags of sand
Oft jerks the string from leaders hand
And on the road will eager stoop
To pick the sprouting thistle up
Oft answering on his weary way
Some distant neighbours sobbing bray
Din[n]ing the ears of driving boy
As if he felt a fit of joy
Wi in its pinfold circle left
Of all its company bereft
Starvd stock no longer noising round
Lone in the nooks of foddering ground
Each skeleton of lingering stack
By winters tempests beaten black
Nodds upon props or bolt upright
Stands swarthy in the summer light
And oer the green grass seems to lower
Like stump of old time wasted tower
All that in winter lookd for hay
Spread from their batterd haunts away
To pick the grass or lye at lare
Beneath the mild hedge shadows there
Sweet month that gives a welcome call
To toil and nature and to all
Yet one day mid thy many joys
Is dead to all its sport and noise
Old may day where's thy glorys gone
All fled and left thee every one
Thou comst to thy old haunts and homes
Unnoticd as a stranger comes

MAY

No flowers are pluckt to hail the[e] now
Nor cotter seeks a single bough
The maids no more on thy sweet morn
Awake their thresholds to adorn
Wi dewey flowers—May locks new come
And princifeathers cluttering bloom
And blue bells from the woodland moss
And cowslip cucking balls to toss
Above the garlands swinging hight
Hang in the soft eves sober light
These maid and child did yearly pull
By many a folded apron full
But all is past the merry song
Of maidens hurrying along
To crown at eve the earliest cow
Is gone and dead and silent now
The laugh raisd at the mocking thorn
Tyd to the cows tail last that morn
The kerchief at arms length displayd
Held up by pairs of swain and maid
While others bolted underneath
Bawling loud wi panting breath
'Duck under water' as they ran
Alls ended as[1] they ne'er began
While the new thing that took thy place
Wears faded smiles upon its face
And where enclosure has its birth
It spreads a mildew oer her mirth
The herd no longer one by one

[1] = as if.

MAY

Goes plodding on her morning way
And garlands lost and sports nigh gone
Leaves her like thee a common day
Yet summer smiles upon thee still
Wi natures sweet unalterd will
And at thy births unworshipd hours
Fills her green lap wi swarms of flowers
To crown thee still as thou hast been
Of spring and summer months the queen

JUNE

Now summer is in flower and natures hum
Is never silent round her sultry bloom
Insects as small as dust are never done
Wi' glittering dance and reeling in the sun
And green wood fly and blossom haunting bee
Are never weary of their melody
Round field hedge now flowers in full glory twine
Large bindweed bells wild hop and streakd woodbine
That lift athirst their slender throated flowers
Agape for dew falls and for honey showers

These round each bush in sweet disorder run
And spread their wild hues to the sultry sun
Where its silk netting lace on twigs and leaves
The mottld spider at eves leisure weaves
That every morning meet the poets eye
Like faireys dew wet dresses hung to dry
The wheat swells into ear and leaves below
The may month wild flowers and their gaudy show
Bright carlock bluecap and corn poppy red
Which in such clouds of colors wid[e]ly spread
That at the sun rise might to fancys eye
Seem to reflect the many colord sky
And leverets seat and lark and partridge nest
It leaves a schoolboys height in snugger rest
And oer the weeders labour overgrows
Who now in merry groups each morning goes
To willow skirted meads wi fork and rake
The scented hay cocks in long rows to make
Where their old visitors in russet brown
The haytime butterflyes dance up and down
And gads that teaze like whasps the timid maid
And drive the herdboys cows to pond and shade
Who when his dogs assistance fails to stop
Is forcd his half made oaten pipes to drop
And start and halloo thro the dancing heat
To keep their gadding tumult from the wheat
Who in their rage will dangers overlook
And leap like hunters oer the pasture brook
Brushing thro blossomd beans in maddening haste
And 'stroying corn they scarce can stop to taste

Labour pursues its toil in weary mood
And feign woud rest wi shadows in the wood
The mowing gangs bend oer the beeded grass
Where oft the gipseys hungry journeying ass
Will turn its wishes from the meadow paths
Listning the rustle of the falling swaths
The ploughman sweats along the fallow vales
And down the suncrackt furrow slowly trails
Oft seeking when athirst the brooks supply
Where brushing eager the brinks bushes bye
For coolest water he oft brakes[1] the rest
Of ring dove brooding oer its idle nest
And there as loath to leave the swaily place
He'll stand to breath and whipe his burning face
The shepherds idle hours are over now
Nor longer leaves him neath the hedgrow bough
On shadow pillowd banks and lolling stile
Wilds looses now their summer friends awhile
Shrill whistles barking dogs and chiding scold
Drive bleating sheep each morn from fallow fold
To wash pits where the willow shadows lean
Dashing them in their fold staind coats to clean
Then turnd on sunning sward to dry agen
They drove them homeward to the clipping pen
In hurdles pent where elm or sycamore
Shut out the sun—or in some threshing floor
There they wi scraps of songs and laugh and tale
Lighten their anual toils while merry ale
Goes round and gladdens old mens hearts to praise
The thread bare customs of old farmers days

[1] = breaks.

Who while the sturting sheep wi trembling fears
Lies neath the snipping of his harmless sheers
Recalls full many a thing by bards unsung
And pride forgot—that reignd when he was young
How the hugh bowl was in the middle set
At breakfast time as clippers yearly met
Filld full of frumity where yearly swum
The streaking sugar and the spotting plumb
Which maids coud never to the table bring
Without one rising from the merry ring
To lend a hand who if twas taen amiss
Woud sell his kindness for a stolen kiss
The large stone pitcher in its homly trim
And clouded pint horn wi its copper rim
Oer which rude healths was drank in spirits high
From the best broach the cellar woud supply
While sung the ancient swains in homly ryhmes
Songs that were pictures of the good old times
When leathern bottles held the beer nut brown
That wakd the sun wi songs and sung him down
Thus will the old man ancient ways bewail
Till toiling sheers gain ground upon the tale
And brakes it off—when from the timid sheep
The fleece is shorn and wi a fearfull leap
He starts—while wi a pressing hand
His sides are printed by the tarry brand
Shaking his naked skin wi wondering joys
And fresh ones are tugd in by sturdy boys
Who when theyre thrown down neath the sheering
　　　swain
Will wipe his brow and start his tale again

Tho fashions haughty frown hath thrown aside
Half the old forms simplicity supplyd
Yet their[1] are some prides winter deigns to spare
Left like green ivy when the trees are bare
And now when sheering of the flocks are done
Some ancient customs mixd wi harmless fun
Crowns the swains merry toils—the timid maid
Pleasd to be praisd and yet of praise affraid
Seeks her best flowers not those of woods and fields
But such as every farmers garden yield
Fine cabbage roses painted like her face
And shining pansys trimmd in golden lace
And tall tuft larkheels featherd thick wi flowers
And woodbines climbing oer the door in bowers
And London tufts of many a mottld hue
And pale pink pea and monkshood darkly blue
And white and purple jiliflowers that stay
Lingering in blossom summer half away
And single blood walls of a lucious smell
Old fashiond flowers which huswives love so well
And columbines stone blue or deep night brown
Their honey-comb-like blossoms hanging down
Each cottage gardens fond adopted child
Tho heaths still claim them where they yet grow
    wild
Mong their old wild companions summer blooms
Furze brake and mozzling ling and golden broom
Snap dragons gaping like to sleeping clowns
And 'clipping pinks' (which maidens sunday gowns

----

[1] = there.

Full often wear catcht at by tozing chaps)
Pink as the ribbons round their snowy caps
'Bess in her bravery' too of glowing dyes
As deep as sunsets crimson pillowd skyes
And majoram notts sweet briar and ribbon grass
And lavender the choice of every lass
And sprigs of lads love all familiar names
Which every garden thro the village claims
These the maid gathers wi a coy delight
And tyes them up in readiness for night
Giving to every swain tween love and shame
Her 'clipping poseys' as their yearly claim
And turning as he claims the custom kiss
Wi stifld smiles half ankering after bliss
She shrinks away and blushing calls it rude
But turns to smile and hopes to be pursued
While one to whom the seeming hint applied
Follows to claim it and is not denyd
No doubt a lover for within his coat
His nosegay owns each flower of better sort
And when the envious mutter oer their beer
And nodd the secret to his neighbor near
Raising the laugh to make the mutter known
She blushes silent and will not disown
And ale and songs and healths and merry ways
Keeps up a shadow of old farmers days
But the old beachen bowl that once supplyd
Its feast of frumity is thrown aside
And the old freedom that was living then
When masters made them merry wi their men

Whose coat was like his neighbors russet brown
And whose rude speech was vulgar as his clown
Who in the same horn drank the rest among
And joind the chorus while a labourer sung
All this is past—and soon may pass away
The time torn remnant of the holiday
As proud distinction makes a wider space
Between the genteel and the vulgar race
Then must they fade as pride oer custom showers
Its blighting mildew on her feeble flowers

JULY

Daughter of pastoral smells and sights
And sultry days and dewy nights
July resumes her yearly place
Wi her milking maiden face
Ruddy and tand yet sweet to view
When everywhere's a vale of dew
And raps[1] it round her looks that smiles
A lovly rest to daily toils
Wi last months closing scenes and dins
Her sultry beaming birth begins

Hay makers still in grounds appear
And some are thinning nearly clear

[1] = wraps.

Save oddly lingering shocks about
Which the tithman counteth out
Sticking their green boughs where they go
The parsons yearly claims to know
Which farmers view wi grudging eye
And grumbling drive their waggons bye
In hedge bound close and meadow plains
Stript groups of busy bustling swains
From all her hants wi noises rude
Drives to the wood lands solitude
That seeks a spot unmarkd wi paths
Far from the close and meadow swaths
Wi smutty song and story gay
They cart the witherd smelling hay
Boys loading on the waggon stand
And men below wi sturdy hand
Heave up the shocks on lathy prong
While horse boys lead the team along
And maidens drag the rake behind
Wi light dress shaping to the wind
And trembling locks of curly hair
And snow white bosoms nearly bare
That charms ones sight amid the hay
Like lingering blossoms of the may
From clowns rude jokes they often turn
And oft their cheeks wi blushes burn
From talk which to escape a sneer
They oft affect as not to hear
Some in the nooks about the ground
Pile up the stacks swelld bellying round

JULY

The milking cattles winter fare
That in the snow are fodderd there
Warm spots wi black thorn thickets lind
And trees to brake[1] the northern wind
While masters oft the sultry hours
Will urge their speed and talk of showers
When boy from home trotts to the stack
Wi dinner upon dobbins back
And bottles to the saddle tyd
Or ballancd upon either side
A horse thats past his toiling day
Yet still a favorite in his way
That trotts on errands up and down
The fields and too and fro from town
Long ere his presence comes in sight
Boys listen wi heart felt delight
And know his footsteps down the road
Hastening wi the dinner load
Then they seek in close or meadows
High hedgerows wi grey willow shadows
To hide beneath from sultry noon
And rest them at their dinner boon
Where helping shepherd for the lass
Will seek a hillock on the grass
The thickset hedge or stack beside
Where teazing pismires ne'er abide
And when tis found down drops the maid
Proud wi the kind attention paid
And still the swain wi notice due
Waits on her all the dinner through

[1] = break.

And fills her horn which she tho dry
In shoyness often pushes bye
While he will urge wi many a smile
It as a strength to help her toil
And in her hand will oft contrive
From out his pocket pulld to slive
Stole fruit when no one turns his eye
To wet her mouth when shes adry
Offerd when she refuses ale
Noons sultry labour to regale
Teazd wi the countless multitude
Of flyes that every where intrude
While boys wi boughs will often try
To beat them from them as they lye
Who find their labour all in vain
And soon as scard they swarm again
Thus while each swain and boy and lass
Sit at their dinner on the grass
The teams wi gears thrown on their backs
Stand pulling at the shocks or racks
Switching their tails and turning round
To knap the gadflys teazing wound
While dob that brought the dinners load
Too tricky to be turnd abroad
Needing the scuttle shook wi grain
To coax him to be caught again
Is to a tree at tether tyd
Ready for boy to mount and ride
Nipping the grass about his pound
And stamping battering hooves around

Soon as each ground is clear of hay
The shepherd whoops his flocks away
From fallow fields to plentys scenes
Shining as smooth as bowling greens
But scard wi clipping tides alarms
They bleat about the close in swarms
And hide neath hedges in the cool
Still panting tho wi out their whool
Markd wi the tard brands lasting dye
And make a restless hue and cry
Answering the lambs that call again
And for their old dams seek in vain
Running mid the stranger throng
And ever meeting wi the wrong
Fiegn[1] wi some old yoe to abide
Who smells and tosses them aside
And some as if they know its face
Will meet a lamb wi mended pace
But proving hopes indulgd in vain
They turn around and blair again
Till weand from memory half forgot
They spread and feed and notice not
Save now and then to lambs shrill crys
Odd yoes in hoarser tone replys
Still may be seen the mowing swain
On balks between the fields of grain
Who often stops his thirst to ease
To pick the juicy pods of pease
And oft as chances bring to pass
Stoops oer his scythe stuck in the grass

[1] = Feign = Fain.

74

To seek the brimming honey comb
Which bees so long were toiling home
And rifld from so many flowers
And carried thro so many hours
He tears their small hives mossy ball
Where the brown labourers hurded all
Who gather homward one by one
And see their nest and honey gone
Humming around his rushing toil
Their mellancholly wrongs awhile
Then oer the sweltering swaths they stray
And hum disconsolate away
And oft neath hedges cooler screen
Where meadow sorrel lingers green
Calld 'sour grass' by the knowing clown
The mower gladly chews it down
And slakes his thirst the best he may
When singing brooks are far away
And his hoopd bottle woeful tale
Is emptied of its cheering ale
That lulld him in unconsious sleep
At dinners hour beneath a heap
Of grass or bush or edding shock
Till startld by the country clock
That told the hours his toil had lost
Who coud but spare an hour at most
And wearing past the setting sun
He stays to get his labour done
The gipsey down the meadow brook
Wi long pole and [a] reaping hook

JULY

Tyd at its end amid the streams
That glitters wi the hot sunbeams
Reaches and cuts the bulrush down
And hawks them round each neighboring town
Packd at his back or tyd in loads
On asses down the dusty roads
He jogs and shouts from door to door
His well known note of calling oer
Offering to huswives cheap repairs
Mending their broken bottomd chairs
Wi step half walk half dance, and eye
Ready to smile on passers bye
Wi load well suiting weather warm
Tuckd carlessly beneath his arm
Or peeping coat and side between
In woolen bag of faded green
Half conseald and half displayd
A purpose tell tale to his trade
The gipsey fiddler jogs away
To village feast and holiday
Scraping in public house to trye
What beer his music will supply
From clowns who happy wi the din
Dance their hand naild hilos thin
Along the roads in passing crowds
Followd by dust like smoaking clouds
Scotch droves of beast a little breed
In swelterd weary mood proceed
A patient race from scottish hills
To fatten by our pasture rills

Lean wi the wants of mountain soil
But short and stout for travels toil
Wi cockd up horns and curling crown
And dewlap bosom hanging down
Followd by slowly pacing swains
Wild to our rushy flats and plains
At whom the shepherds dog will rise
And shake himself and in supprise
Draw back and waffle in affright
Barking the traveller out of sight
And mowers oer their scythes will bear
Upon their uncooth dress to stare
And shepherds as they trample bye
Leaves oer their hooks a wondering eye
To witness men so oddly clad
In petticoats of banded plad
Wi blankets oer their shoulders slung
To camp at night the fields among
When they for rest on commons stop
And blue cap like a stocking top
Cockt oer their faces summer brown
Wi scarlet tazzeles on the crown
Rude patterns of the thistle flower
Untrickd and open to the shower
And honest faces fresh and free
That breath[e] of mountain liberty
The pindar on the sabbath day
Soon as the darkness waxes grey
Before one sun beam oer the ground
Spindles its light and shadow round

Goes round the fields at early morn
To see what stock are in the corn
To see what chances sheep may win
Thro gaps the gipsey pilfers thin
Or if theyve forcd a restless way
By rubbing at a loosend tray
Or nuzling colt that trys to catch
A gate at night left off the latch
By traveller seeking home in haste
Or the clown by fareys chas'd
That listning while he makes a stand
Opens each gate wi fearful hand
And dreads a minute to remain
To put it on the latch again
And cows who often wi their horns
Toss from the gaps the stuffing thorns
These like a fox upon the watch
He in the morning tryes to catch
And drives them to the pound for pay
Carless about the sabbath day
Soon as the morning wakens red
The shepherd startles from his bed
And rocks afield his moving pace
While[1] folded sheep will know his face
Rising as he appears in sight
To shake their coats as in delight
His shadow stalking stride for stride
Stretches a jiant by his side
Long as a tree without a top
And oft it urges him to stop

[1] See Glossary.

Both in his journey and his song
And wonders why it seems so long
And bye and bye as morning dies
Shrinks to an unbrichd boy in size
Then as the evening gathers blue
Grows to a jiants length anew
Puzzld the more he stops to pause
His wisdom vainly seeks the cause
Again his journey he pursues
Lengthening his track along the dews
And his dog that turnd to pick
From his sides the sucking tick
Insects that on cattle creep
And bites the labourer laid asleep
Pricks up his ears to see twas gone
And shakes his hide and hastens on
And the while the shepherd stayd
Trailing a track the hare had made
Bolts thro the creeping hedge again
And hurring[1] follows wi the swain
The singing shouting herding boys
Follows again their wild employs
And ere the sun puts half his head
From out his crimson pillowd bed
And bawls behind his cows again
That one by one lobs down the lane
Wi wild weeds in his hat anew
The summer sorts of every hue
And twigs of leaves that please his eye
To his old haunts he hallows bye

[1] = hurrying.

Wi dog that loiters by his side
Or trotts before wi nimble stride
That waits till bid to bark and run
And panteth from the dreaded sun
And oft amid the sunny day
Will join a partner in his play
And in his antic tricks and glee
Will prove as fond of sport as he
And by the flag pool summer warm
He'll watch the motions of his arm
That holds a stick or stone to throw
In the sun gilded flood below
And head oer ears he danses in
Nor fears to wet his curly skin
The boys field cudgel to restore
And brings it in his mouth ashore
And eager as for crust or bone
He'll run to catch the pelted stone
Till wearied out he shakes his hide
And drops his tail and sneaks aside
Unheeding whistles shouts and calls
To take a rest where thickly falls
The rush clumps shadows there he lyes
Licking his skin and catching flyes
Or picking tween his stretching feet
The bone he had not time to eat
Before when wi the teazing boy
He was so throngd wi plays employ
Noon gathers wi its blistering breath
Around and day dyes still as death

JULY

The breeze is stopt the lazy bough
Hath not a leaf that dances now
The totter grass upon the hill
And spiders threads is hanging still
The feathers dropt from morehens wings
Upon the waters surface clings
As stedfast and as heavy seem
As stones beneath them in the stream
Hawkweed and groundsels fairey downs
Unruffld keep their seeding crowns
And in the oven heated air
Not one light thing is floating there
Save that to the earnest eye
The restless heat swims twittering bye
The swine run restless down the street
Anxious some pond or ditch to meet
From days hot swoonings to retire
Wallowing in the weeds and mire
The linnets seek the twiggs that lye
Close to the brook and brig stones drye
At top and sit and dip their bills
Till they have drunk their little fills
Then flurt their wings and wet their feathers
To cool them in the blazing weathers
Dashing the water oer their heads
Then high[1] them to some cooling sheds
Where dark wood glooms about the plain
To pick their feathers smooth again
The young quick's branches seem as dead
And scorch from yellow into red

[1] = hie.

Ere autumn hath its pencil taen
Their shades in different hues to stain
Following behind the crawling ploughs
Whiping oft their sweating brows
The boys lead horses yokd in pairs
To jumping harrows linkd that tears
And teazes the hard clods to dust
Placing for showers in hopes their trust
The farmer follows sprinkling round
Wi turnip seed the panting ground
Providing food for beast and sheep
When winters snows are falling deep
Oft proving hopes and wishes vain
While clouds disperse that promisd rain
When soon as ere the turnip creeps
From out the crust burnt soil and peeps
Upon the farmers watching eye
Tis eaten by the jumping flye
And eager neath the midday sun
Soon as each plough teams toil is done
Scarse waiting till the gears are taen
From off their backs by boy and swain
From hayfilld racks they turn away
Nor in the stable care to stay
Hurr[y]ing to the trough to drink
Or from the yard ponds muddy brink
Rush in and wi long winded soak
Drink till theyre almost fit to choak
And from the horsbees teazing din
Thrust deep their burning noses in

Almost above their greedy eyes
To cool their mouths and shun the flyes
Deaf to the noise the geese will make
That grudge the worthy share they take
Boys now neath green lanes meeting bough
Each noons half holiday from plough
Take out their hungry teams till night
That nipp the grass wi eager bite
Wi long tails switching never still
They lounge neath trees when eat their fill
And stamp and switch till closing day
Brushing the teazing flyes away
Endless labour all in vain
That start in crowds to turn again
When the sun is sinking down
And dyes more deep the shadows brown
And gradual into slumber glooms
How sweet the village evening comes
To weary hinds from toil releasd
And panting sheep and torturd beast
The shepherd long wi heat opprest
Betakes him to his cottage rest
And his tird dog that plods along
Wi panting breath and lolling tongue
Runs eager as the brook appears
And dashes in head over ears
Startling reed sparrow broods to flye
That in the reed woods slumberd nigh
And water rotts in haste to hide
Nibbling the sedges close beside

Lapping while he floats about
To quench his thirst then drabbles out
And shakes his coat and like the swain
Is happy night is come again

The beast that to the pond did creep
And rushd in water belly deep
The gad flyes threatning hums to shun
And horse bee darting in the sun
Lashing their tails the while they stood
And sprinkling thick their sides wi mud
Snuff the cool air now day is gone
And linger slow and idly on
To the pebbly fore to drink
And drop and rest upon its brink
Ruminating on their beds
Calm as the sky above their heads
The horse whose mouth is seldom still
Is up and cropping at his will
The moisting grass unteazd and free
In summer eves serenity
Uncheckt by flyes he grazes on
Right happy that the day is gone
Ne'er leaving off to turn around
His stooping head to knap the wound
And tail that switchd his sides all day
Is quiet now the suns away
The cowboys as their herd plod on
Before them homward one by one
Grows happy as their toil grows short
And full of fancys restless sport

Oft starts along wi sinking day
Acting proud their soldier play
Wi peeld bark sash around each waist
And rush caps oer each beaver placd
Stuck wi a headaches red cockade
And wooden swords and sticks displayd
For flags—thus march the evening troop
While soon one strikes a whistle up
And others wi their dinner tins
The evenings falling quiet dins
Patting wi hollow sounding tums
And imitating pipes and drums
Calling their cows that plod before
Their army marching from the moor
And thus they act till met the town
Carless of laughs from passing clown
Even their dogs too tird for play
Loiter on their evening way
Oft rolling on the damping grass
Or stopping wi the milking lass
Waiting a chance the ways conseal
A mouth full from her pails to steal
Dropping down to pick a bone
The hedger from his wallets thrown
Or found upon some greensward platt
Where hayfolks at their dinner sat
Sweet the cows breath down the lane
Steaming the fragrance of the plain
As home they rock and bawling wait
Till boys run to unloose the gate

And from their milksheds all adry
Turn to the pump wi anxious eye
Where shoud the maids wi boys repair
To fill the dashing bucket there
They hurry spite of threatning clown
And kick the milkers bucket down
And horses oft wi eager stoop
Will bend adown to steal a sup
Watching a moments chance to win
And dip their eager noses in
As by they pass or set it down
To rest or chatter to a clown
And knats wi their small slender noise
Bother too the troubld boys
And teaze the cows that while she chides
Will kick and turn to lick their sides
And like so many hanting sprites
Will bite and weal the maid anights
Who dreams of love and sleeps so sound
As ne'er to feel each little wound
Till waken by the morning sun
She wonders at the injury done
Thinking in fears simplicity
That faireys dreaded mistery
On her white bosom in the dark
Had been and left each blisterd mark
The fox begins his stunt odd bark
Down in its dew bed drops the lark
And on the heath amid the gorse
The night hawk stints the feeding horse

That pricks his ear wi startling eye
And snorts to hear its trembling crye
The owlet leaves his ivy tree
Into its hive slow sails the bee
The mower seeks his cloaths and hides
His scythe home bent wi weary strides
And oer his shoulder swings his bag
Bearing in hand his empty cag
Hay makers on their homward way
Into the fields will often stray
Among the grain when no one sees
Nestle and fill their laps wi peas
Sheep scard wi tweenlight doubting eye
Leap the path and canter bye
Nipping wi moment stoops the plain
And turning quick to gaze again
Till silence upon eve awaits
And milkmaids cease to clap the gates
And homward to the town are gone
Wi whispering sweethearts chatting on
And shepherds homward tracks are past
And dogs rude barks are still at last
Then down they drop as suits their wills
Or nips the thyme on pismire hills
Where nought is seen but timid hares
That nights sweet welcome gladly shares
And shadows stooping as they stoop
Beside them when the moon gets up
Reviving wi the ruddy moon
The nightingale resumes his tune

JULY

What time the horsboy drives away
His loose teams from the toils of day
To crop the closes dewy blade
Where the hay stacks fencd and made
Or on the commons bushy plain
To rest till the sun comes again
Whistling and bawling loud and long
The burthen of some drawling song
That grows more loud as eve grows late
Yet when he opes the clapping gate
He cant help turning in his joys
To look if his fear damping noise
Has raisd a mischief in the wind
And wakd a ghost to stalk behind
And when hes turnd them safe aground
And hookd the chain the gate around
Wi quicker speed he homward sings
And leaves them in the mushroom rings
Wi the dewdrunk dancing elves
To eat or rest as suits themselves
And as he hastes from labour done
An owlets whoop een makes him run
And bats shill flickerings bobbing near
Turns his heart blood cold wi fear
And when at home wi partner ralph
He hugs himself to think hes safe
And tells his tale while others smile
Of all he thought and feard the while
The black house bee hath ceasd to sing
And white nosd one wi out a sting

That boys will catch devoid of dread
Are in their little holes abed
And martins neath the mossey eves
Oft startld at the sparrow thieves
That in their house will often peep
Breaking their little weary sleep
And oft succeed when left alone
In making their clay huts their own
Where the cock sparrow on the scout
Watches and keeps the owner out
The geese have left the home close moats
And at the yard gate clean their coats
Or neath their feathers tuck their heads
Asleep till driven to their sheds
The pigeon droves in whisking flight
Hurrying to their coats[1] ere night
In coveys round the village meet
And in the dove coat holes retreat
Nor more about the wheaten grounds
The bird boys bell and clapper sounds
Retiring wi the setting sun
His toil and shout and song is done
The shrill bat wi its flitting mate
Starts thro the church vaults iron grate
Deaths daily visitors and all
He meets save slanting suns that fall
At eve as if they lovd to shed
Their daily memory oer the dead

---

[1] = cotes.

Hodge neath the climbing elms that drop
Their branches oer a dove coat top
Hath milkd his cows and taken in
On yokes the reeking pales or tin
And been across the straw to chain
The hen roost wicket safe again
And done his yard rounds hunting eggs
And taen his hat from off the peggs
To scamper to the circling cross
To have a game at pitch and toss
And day boy hath his supper got
Of milk before twas hardly hot
Eager from toil to get away
And join the boys at taw to play
Neath black smiths cinder litterd shed
Till the hour to go to bed
Old gossips on the greensward bench
Sit where the hombound milking wench
Will set her buckets down to rest
And be awhile their evening guest
To whom their box is held while she
Takes the smallest nips that be
That soon as snift begins to teaze
And makes her turn away to sneeze
While old dames say the sign is plain
That she will dream about her swain
And toss the cloaths from off her bed
And cautions her of roguish ned
Holding their hands agen their hips
To laugh as up she starts and trips

In quickend speed along the town
Bidding good night to passing clown

From the black smiths shop the swain
Jogs wi ploughshares laid again
And drops them by the stable shed
Where gears on pegs hang over head
Ready for driving boys to take
On fore horse when their toils awake
The kitchen wench wi face red hot
As blazing fire neath supper pot
Hath cleand her pails and pansions all
And set them leaning by the wall
And twirld her whool mop clean again
And hung it on the pales to drain

Now by the maids requesting smile
The shepherd mounts the wood stack pile
Reard high against the orchard pales
And cause of thorns she oft bewails
Prickd hands and holes in sunday gown
He throws the smoothest faggot down
And hawls it in at her desire
Ready for the kitching fire

Beneath the elderns village shade
Oer her well curb leans the maid
To draw the brimming bucket up
While passing boy to beg a sup
Will stop his roll or rocking cart
And the maidens gentle heart

91

Gives ready leave—the eager clown
Throws off his hat and stoops adown
Soaking his fill then hastens on
To catch his team already gone
Eager from toil to get release
And in the hay field feed at peace

The weary thresher leaves his barn
And emptys from his shoes the corn
That gatherd in them thro the day
And homward bends his weary way
The gardener he is sprinkling showers
From watering pans on drooping flowers
And set away his hoe and spade
While goody neath the cottage shade
Sits wi a baskett tween her knees
Ready for supper shelling peas
And cobler chatting in the town
Hath put his window shutter down
And the knowing parish clerk
Feign to do his jobs ere dark
Hath timd the church clock to the sun
And wound it up for night and done
And turnd the hugh key in the door
Chatting his evening story oer
Up the street the servant maid
Runs wi her errands long delayd
And ere the door she enters in
She stops to right a loosend pin
And smooth wi hasty fingers down
The crumpling creases in her gown

Which Rogers oggles rudly made
For may games forfeit never paid
And seizd a kiss against her will
While playing quoits upon the hill
Wi other shepherds laughing nigh
That made her shoy and hurry bye
The blacksmiths gangling toil is oer
And shut his hot shops branded door
Folding up his arms to start
And take at ease his evening quart
And farmer giles his business done
Wi face a very setting sun
Jogging home on dobbins back
From helping at the clover stack
The horse knows well nor trys to pass
The door where for his custom glass
He nightly from the saddle jumps
To slake his thirst or cheer the dumps
Leaving old dob his breath to catch
Wi bridle hanging at the latch
The shepherd too will often spare
A sixpence to be merry there
While the dog that trackd his feet
Adown the dusty printed street
Lies as one weary loath to roam
Agen the door to wait him home
While the taylors long day thirst
Is still unquenchd tho fit to burst
Whose[1] been at truants merry play
From sheers and bodkin all the day

[1] = who's.

Still soaks the tankard reeling ripe
And scarce can stoop to light his pipe
The labourer sitting by his door
Happy that the day is oer
Is stooping downwards to unloose
His leathern baffles or his shoes
Making ready for his rest
Quickly to be the pillows guest
While on mothers lap wi in
The childern each their prayers begin
That taen from play are loath to go
And looking round repeating slow
Each prayer they stammer in delay
To gain from bed a longer stay
Goody hath set her spinning bye
Deafend by her chattering pye
That calls her up wi hungry rage
To put his supper in the cage
That done she sought a neighbours door
A minutes time to gossip oer
And neath her apron now tis night
Huddles for home, her candle light
Hid from the wind—to burn an hour
As clouds wi threatend thunder lower
The mastiff from his kennel free
Is now unchaind at liberty
In readiness to put to rout
The thieves that night may bring about
Thus evening deepning to a close
Leaves toil and nature to repose

AUGUST

Harvest approaches with its bustling day
The wheat tans brown and barley bleaches grey
In yellow garb the oat land intervenes
And tawney glooms the valley thronged with beans
Silent the village grows, wood wandering dreams
Seem not so lovely as its quiet seems
Doors are shut up as on a winters day
And not a child about them lies at play
The dust that winnows neath the breezes feet
Is all that stirs about the silent street
Fancy might think that desert spreading fear
Had whisperd terrors into quiets ear

Or plundering armys past the place had come
And drove the lost inhabitants from home
The fields now claim them where a motley crew
Of old and young their daily tasks pursue
The barleys beard is grey and wheat is brown
And wakens toil betimes to leave the town
The reapers leave their beds before the sun
And gleaners follow when home toils are done
To pick the littered ear the reaper leaves
And glean in open fields among the sheaves
The ruddy child nursed in the lap of care
In toils rude ways to do its little share
Beside its mother poddles oer the land
Sun burnt and stooping with a weary hand
Picking its tiney glean of corn or wheat
While crackling stubbles wound its legs and feet
Full glad it often is to sit awhile
Upon a smooth green baulk to ease its toil
And feign would spend an idle hour to play
With insects strangers to the moiling day
Creeping about each rush and grassy stem
And often wishes it was one of them
In weariness of heart that it might lye
Hid in the grass from the days burning eye
That raises tender blisters on his skin
Thro holes or openings that have lost a pin
Free from the crackling stubs to toil and glean
And smiles to think how happy it had been
Whilst its expecting mother stops to tye
Her handful up and waiting his supply

Misses the resting younker from her side
And shouts of rods and morts of threats beside
Pointing to the grey willows while she tells
His fears shall fetch one if he still rebells
Picturing harsh truths in its unpracticed eye
How they who idle in the harvest lye
Shall well deserving in the winter pine
Or hunt the hedges with the birds and swine
In vain he wishes that the rushes height
Were tall as trees to hide him from her sight
Leaving his pleasant seat he sighs and rubs
His legs and shows scratchd wounds from piercing
    stubs
To make excuse for play but she disdains
His little wounds and smiles while he complains
And as he stoops adown in troubles sore
She sees his grief and bids him sob no more
As bye and bye on the next sabbath day
She'll give him well earned pence as well as play
When he may buy almost with out a stint
Sweet candied horehound cakes and pepper mint
Or streaking sticks of lusious lolipop
What ere he chuses from the tempting shop
Wi in whose diamond winder shining lye
Things of all sorts to tempt his eager eye
Rich sugar plumbs in phials shining bright
In every hue young fancys to delight
Coaches and ladys of gilt ginger bread
And downy plumbs and apples streaked with red
Such promises all sorrows soon displace
And smiles are instant kindled in his face

Scorning all troubles which he felt before
He picks the trailing ears and mourns no more
The fields are all alive with busy noise
Of labours sounds and insects humming joys
Some oer the glittering sickle sweating stoop
Startling full oft the partridge coveys up
Some oer the rustling scythe go bending on
And shockers follow where their toils have gone
First turning swaths to wither in the sun
Where mice from terrors dangers nimbly run
Leaving their tender young in fears alarm
Lapt up in nests of chimbled grasses warm
And oft themselves for safty search in vain
From the rude boy or churlish hearted swain
Who beat their stone chinkd forks about the ground
And spread an instant murder all around
Tho oft the anxious maidens tender prayer
Urges the clown their little lives to spare
Who sighs while trailing the long rake along
At scenes so cruel and forgets her song
And stays wi love his murder aiming hand
Some ted the puffing winnow down the land
And others following roll them up in heaps
While cleanly as a barn door beesome sweeps
The hawling drag wi gathering weeds entwind
And singing rakers end the toils behind

When the sun stoops to meet the western sky
And noons hot hours have wanderd weary bye
They seek an awthorn bush or willow tree
Or stouk or shock where coolest shadows be

Where baskets heapd and unbroachd bottles lye
Which dogs in absence watchd with wary eye
To catch their breath awhile and share the boon
Which beavering time alows their toil at noon
All gathering sit on stubbs or sheaves the hour
Where scarlet poppys linger still in flower
Stript in his shirt the hot swain drops adown
And close beside him in her unpind gown
Next to her favoured swain the maiden steals
Blushing at kindness which her love reveals
Who makes a seat for her of things around
And drops beside her on the naked ground
Wearied wi brambles catching at her gown
And pulling nutts from branches pulld adown
By friendly swain the maid wi heaving breast
Upon her lovers shoulder leans at rest
Then from its cool retreat the beer they bring
And hand the stout hooped bottle round the ring
Each swain soaks hard—the maiden ere she sips
Shrieks at the bold whasp settling on her lips
That seems determined only hers to greet
As if it fancied they were cherrys sweet
So dog forgoes his sleep awhile or play
Springing at frogs that rustling jump away
To watch each morsel that the boon bestows
And wait the bone or crumb the shepherd throws
For shepherds are no more of ease possest
But share the harvests labours with the rest

When day declines and labour meets repose
The bawling boy his evening journey goes

At toils unwearied call the first and last
He drives his horses to their nights repast
In dewey close or meadow to sojourn
And often ventures on his still return
Oer garden pales or orchard walls to hie
When sleeps safe key hath locked up dangers eye
All but the mastiff watching in the dark
Who snufts and knows him and forbears to bark
With fearful haste he climbs each loaded tree
And picks for prizes which the ripest be
Pears plumbs or filberts covered oer in leams
While the pale moon creeps high in peaceful dreams
And oer his harvest theft in jealous light
Fills empty shadows with the power to fright
And owlet screaming as it bounces nigh
That from some barn hole pops and hurries bye
Scard at the cat upon her nightly watch
For rats that come for dew upon the thatch
He hears the noise and trembling to escape
While every object grows a dismal shape
Drops from the tree in fancys swiftest dread
By ghosts pursued and scampers home to bed
Quick tumbling oer the mossy mouldering wall
And looses half his booty in the fall
Where soon as ere the morning opes its eyes
The restless hogs will happen on the prize
And crump adown the mellow and the green
And makes all seem as nothing ne'er had been
Amid the broils of harvests weary reign
How sweet the sabbath wakes its rest again

AUGUST

For each weary mind what rapture dwells
To hear once more its pleasant chiming bells
That from each steeple peeping here and there
Murmur a soothing lullaby to care
The shepherd journying on his morning rounds
Pauses awhile to hear their pleasing sounds
While the glad childern free from toils employ
Mimic the ding dong sounds and laugh for joy
The fields themselves seem happy to be free
Where insects chatter with unusual glee
While solitude the stubbs and grass among
Apears to muse and listen to the song

In quiet peace awakes the welcomed morn
Men tired and childern with their gleaning worn
Weary and stiff lye round their doors the day
To rest themselves with little heart for play
No more keck horns in homestead close resounds
As in their school boy days at hare and hounds
Nor running oer the street from wall to wall
With eager shouts at 'cuck and catch the ball'
In calm delight the sabbath wears along
Yet round the cross at noon a tempted throng
Of little younkers with their pence repair
To buy the downy plumb and lucious pear
That melt i' th mouth—which gardners never fail
For gains strong impulse to expose for sale
And on the circling cross steps in the sun
Sit when the parson has his sermon done
When grandams that against his rules rebell
Come wi their baskets heapd wi fruit to sell

That thither all the season did pursue
Wi mellow goosberrys of every hue
Green ruffs and raspberry reds and drops of gold[1]
That makes mouths water often to behold
Sold out to clowns in totts oft deemd too small
Who grudging much the price eat husks and all
Nor leaves a fragment round to cheer the eye
Of searching swine that murmurs hungry bye
And currans red and white on cabbage leaves
While childerns fingers itches to be thieves
And black red cherrys shining to the sight
As rich as brandy held before the light
Now these are past he still as sunday comes
Sits on the cross wi baskets heapd wi plumbs
And Jenitens streakd apples suggar sweet
Others spice scented ripening wi the wheat
And pears that melt ith' mouth like honey which
He oft declares to make their spirits itch
They are so juicy ripe and better still
So rich they een might suck em thro a quill
Here at their leisure gather many a clown
To talk of grain and news about the town
And here the boy wi toils earnd penny comes
In hurrying speed to purchase pears or plumbs
And oer the basket hangs wi many a smile
Wi hat in hand to hold his prize the while

Not so the boys that begs for pence in vain
Of deaf eard dames that threat while they complain

---

[1] These are varieties of gooseberry.

Who talk of the good dinners they have eat
And wanting more as nothing but consiet
Vowing they ne'er shall throw good pence away
So bids them off and be content wi play
Reaching her rod that hangs the chimney oer
And scaring their rude whinings to the door
Who sob aloud and hang their hats adown
To hide their tears and sawn along the town
Venturing wi sullen step his basket nigh
And often dipping a desiring eye
Stone hearted dames thrifts errors to believe
Who make their little bellys yearn to thieve
But strong temptation must to fears resign
For close beside the stocks in terror shine
So choaking substitutes for loss of pelf
He keeps his hungry fingers to himself
And mopes and sits the sabbath hours away
Wi heart too weary and too sad for play
So sundays scenes and leisure passes bye
In rests soft peace and home tranquillity
Till monday morning doth its cares pursue
And wakes the harvests busy toils anew

SEPTEMBER

Harvest awakes the morning still
And toils rude groups the valleys fill
Deserted is each cottage hearth
To all life save the crickets mirth
Each burring wheel their sabbath meets
Nor walks a gossip in the streets
The bench beneath its eldern bough
Lined oer with grass is empty now
Where blackbirds caged from out the sun
Could whistle while their mistress spun

SEPTEMBER

All haunt the thronged fields still to share
The harvests lingering bounty there
As yet no meddling boys resort
About the streets in idle sport
The butterflye enjoys his hour
And flirts unchaced from flower to flower
And humming bees that morning calls
From out the low huts mortar walls
Which passing boy no more controuls
Flye undisturbed about their holes
And sparrows in glad chirpings meet
Unpelted in the quiet street

None but imprison'd childern now
Are seen where dames with angry brow
Threaten each younker to his seat
That thro' the school door eyes the street
Or from his horn book turns away
To mourn for liberty and play
Loud are the mornings early sounds
That farm and cottage yard surrounds
The creaking noise of opening gate
And clanking pumps where boys await
With idle motion to supply
The thirst of cattle crowding bye
The low of cows and bark of dogs
And cackling hens and wineing hogs
Swell high—while at the noise awoke
Old goody seeks her milking cloak
And hastens out to milk the cow
And fill the troughs to feed the sow

Or seeking old hens laid astray
Or from young chickens drives away
The circling kite that round them flyes
Waiting the chance to seize the prize
Hogs trye thro gates the street to gain
And steal into the fields of grain
From nights dull prison comes the duck
Waddling eager thro the muck
Squeezing thro the orchard pales
Where mornings bounty rarely fails
Eager gobbling as they pass
Dew worms thro the padded grass
Where blushing apples round and red
Load down the boughs and pat the head
Of longing maid that hither goes
To hang on lines the drying cloaths
Who views them oft with tempted eye
And steals one as she passes bye
Where the holly oak so tall
Far oer tops the garden wall
That latest blooms for bees provide
Hived on stone benches close beside
The bees their teazing music hum
And threaten war to all that come
Save the old dame whose jealous care
Places a trapping bottle there
Filled with mock sweets in whose disguise
The honey loving hornet dies

Upon the dovecoats mossy slates
The piegons coo around their mates

SEPTEMBER

Where morns sunbeams early fall
By the barn or stable wall
Basking hens in playfull rout
Flap the smoaking dust about
In the barn hole sits the cat
Watching within the thirsty rat
Who oft at morn its dwelling leaves
To drink the moisture from the eves
The redbreast with his nimble eye
Dare scarcely stop to catch the flye
That tangled in the spiders snare
Mourns in vain for freedom there
The dog beside the threshold lyes
Mocking sleep with half shut eyes
With head crouched down upon his feet
Till strangers pass his sunny seat
Then quick he pricks his ears to hark
And bustles up to growl and bark
While boys in fear stop short their song
And sneak on hurrys fears along
And beggar creeping like a snail
To make his hungry hopes prevail
Oer the warm heart of charity
Leaves his lame halt and hastens bye

The maid afield now leaves the farm
With brimming bottles on her arm
Loitering unseen in narrow lane
To be oertook by following swain
Who happy thus her truth to prove
Carrys the load and talks of love

SEPTEMBER

Full soon the harvest waggons sound
Rumbling like thunder all around
In ceasless speed the corn to load
Hurrying down the dusty road
While driving boy with eager eye
Watches the church clock passing bye
Whose gilt hands glitter in the sun
To see how far the hours have run
Right happly in the breathless day
To see it wearing fast away
Yet now and then a sudden shower
Will bring to toil a resting hour
When under sheltering shocks a crowd
Of merry voices mingle loud
Wearing the short lived boon along
With vulgar tale and merry song
Draining with leisures laughing eye
Each welcome bubbling bottle drye
Till peeping suns dry up the rain
Then off they start to toil again

Anon the fields are wearing clear
And glad sounds hum in labours ear
When childern halo[1] 'here they come'
And run to meet the harvest home
Stuck thick with boughs and thronged with
    boys
Who mingle loud a merry noise
Glad that the harvests end is nigh
And weary labour nearly bye

[1] = halloo.

Where when they meet the stack thronged
    yard
Cross bunns or pence their shouts reward

Then comes the harvest supper night
Which rustics welcome with delight
When merry game and tiresome tale
And songs increasing with the ale
Their mingled uproar interpose
To crown the harvests happy close
While rural mirth that there abides
Laughs till she almost cracks her sides

Now harvests busy hum declines
And labour half its help resigns
Boys glad at heart to play return
The shepherds to their peace sojourn
Rush-bosomed solitudes among
Which busy toil disturbed so long
The gossip happy all is oer
Visits again her neighbours door
For scandals idle tales to dwell
Which harvest had no time to tell
And on each bench at even tide
Which trailing vine leaves nearly hide
And free from all its sultry strife
Enjoy once more their idle life
A few whom waning toil reprieves
Thread the forests sea of leaves
Where the pheasant loves to hide
And the darkest glooms abide

Beneath the old oaks mossd and grey
Whose shadows seem as old as they
Where time hath many seasons won
Since aught beneath them saw the sun.
Within these brambly solitudes
The ragged noisy boy intrudes
To gather nuts that ripe and brown
As soon as shook will patter down
Thus harvest ends its busy reign
And leaves the fields their peace again
Where autumns shadows idly muse
And tinge the trees with many hues
Amid whose scenes I'm feign to dwell
And sing of what I love so well
But hollow winds and tumbling floods
And humming showers and moaning woods
All startle into sudden strife
And wake a mighty lay to life
Making amid their strains divine
All songs in vain so mean as mine

OCTOBER

Nature now spreads around in dreary hue
A pall to cover all that summer knew
Yet in the poets solitary way
Some pleasing objects for his praise delay
Somthing that makes him pause and turn again
As every trifle will his eye detain
The free horse rustling through the stubble land
And bawling herd boy with his motly band
Of hogs and sheep and cows who feed their fill
Oer cleard fields rambling where so ere they will

The geese flock gabbling in the splashy fields
And qua[c]king ducks in pondweeds half conseald
Or seeking worms along the homclose sward
Right glad of freedom from the prison yard
While every cart rut dribbles its low tide
And every hollow splashing sports provide
The hedger stopping gaps wi pointed bough
Made by intruding horse and blundering cow
The milk maid tripping on her morning way
And fodderers oft tho early cutting hay
Dropping the littering forkfulls from his back
Side where the thorn fence circles round the stack
The cotter journying wi his noisey swine
Along the wood side where the brambles twine
Shaking from dinted cups the acorns brown
And from the hedges red awes dashing down
And nutters rustling in the yellow woods
Scaring from their snug lairs the pheasant broods
And squirrels secret toils oer winter dreams
Picking the brown nuts from the yellow beams
And hunters from the thickets avenue
In scarlet jackets startling on the view
Skiming a moment oer the russet plain
Then hiding in the colord woods again
The ploping guns sharp momentary shock
Which eccho bustles from her cave to mock
The sticking[1] groups in many a ragged set
Brushing the woods their harmless loads to get
And gipseys camps in some snug shelterd nook
Where old lane hedges like the pasture brook

[1] i.e. stick-gathering.

112

Run crooking as they will by wood and dell
In such lone spots these wild wood roamers dwell
On commons where no farmers claims appear
Nor tyrant justice rides to interfere
Such the abodes neath hedge or spreading oak
And but discovered by its curling smoak
Puffing and peeping up as wills the breeze
Between the branches of the colord trees
Such are the pictures that october yields
To please the poet as he walks the fields
Oft dames in faded cloak of red or grey
Loiters along the mornings dripping way
Wi wicker basket on their witherd arms
Searching the hedges of home close or farms
Where brashy elder trees to autum fade
Each cotters mossy hut and garden shade
Whose glossy berrys picturesquly weaves
Their swathy bunches mid the yellow leaves
Where the pert sparrow stains his little bill
And tutling robin picks his meals at will
Black ripening to the wan suns misty ray
Here the industrious huswives wend their way
Pulling the brittle branches carefull down
And hawking loads of berrys to the town
Wi unpretending skill yet half divine
To press and make their eldern berry wine
That bottld up becomes a rousing charm
To kindle winters icy bosom warm
That wi its merry partner nut brown beer
Makes up the peasants christmass keeping cheer

While nature like fair woman in decay
Which pale consumption hourly wastes away
Upon her waining features pale and chill
Wears dreams of beauty that seem lovely still
Among the heath furze still delights to dwell
Quaking as if with cold the harvest bell
The mushroom buttons each moist morning brings
Like spots of snow in the green tawney rings
And fuzz balls swelld like bladders in the grass
Which oft the merry laughing milking lass
Will stoop to gather in her sportive airs
And slive in mimickd fondness unawares
To smut the brown cheek of the teazing swain
Wi the black powder which their balls contain
Who feigns offence at first that love may speed
Then charms a kiss to recompence the deed
The flying clouds urged on in swiftest pace
Like living things as if they runned a race
The winds that oer each coming tempest broods
Waking like spirits in their startling moods
Fluttering the sear leaves on the blasting lea
That litters under every fading tree
And pausing oft as falls the pattering rain
Then gathering strength and twirling them again
The startld stockdove hurried wizzing bye
As the still hawk hangs oer him in the sky
Crows from the oak trees qawking as they spring
Dashing the acorns down wi beating wing
Waking the woodlands sleep in noises low
Pattring on crimpt brakes withering brown below

114

OCTOBER

While from their hollow nest the squirrels pop
Adown the tree to pick them as they drop
The starnel crowds that dim the muddy light
The crows and jackdaws flapping home at night
And puddock circling round its lazy flight
Round the wild sweeing wood in motion slow
Before it perches on the oaks below
And hugh black beetles revelling alone
In the dull evening with their heavy drone
Buzzing from barn door straw and hovel sides
Where fodderd cattle from the night abides
These pictures linger thro the shortning day
And cheer the lone bards mellancholy way
And now and then a solitary boy
Journeying and muttering oer his dreams of joy

NOVEMBER

The village sleeps in mist from morn till noon
And if the sun wades thro tis wi a face
Beamless and pale and round as if the moon
When done the journey of its nightly race
Had found him sleeping and supplyd his place
For days the shepherds in the fields may be
Nor mark a patch of sky—blindfold they trace
The plains that seem wi out a bush or tree
Whistling aloud by guess to flocks they cannot see

The timid hare seems half its fears to loose
Crouching and sleeping neath its grassy lare

And scarcly startles tho the shepherd goes
Close by its home and dogs are barking there
The wild colt only turns around to stare
At passers bye then naps his hide again
And moody crows beside the road forbeer[1]
To flye tho pelted by the passing swain
Thus day seems turned to night and trys to wake in
    vain

The Owlet leaves her hiding place at noon
And flaps her grey wings in the doubting light
The hoarse jay screams to see her out so soon
And small birds chirp and startle with affright
Much doth it scare the superstitious white[2]
Who dreams of sorry luck and sore dismay
While cow boys think the day a dream of night
And oft grow fearful on their lonly way
Who fancy ghosts may wake and leave their graves
    by day

The cleanly maiden thro the village streets
In pattens clicks down causways never drye
While eves above head drips—where oft she meets
The schoolboy leering on wi mischiefs eye
Trying to splash her as he hurrys bye
While swains afield returning to their ploughs
Their passing aid wi gentle speech apply
And much loves rapture thrills when she alows
Their help wi offerd hand to lead her oer the sloughs

[1] = forbear.   [2] = wight.

NOVEMBER

The hedger soakd wi the dull weather chops
On at his toils which scarcly keeps him warm
And every stroke he takes large swarms of drops
Patter about him like an april storm
The sticking dame wi cloak upon her arm
To guard against a storm walks the wet leas
Of willow groves or hedges round the farm
Picking up aught her splashy wanderings sees
Dead sticks the sudden winds have shook from off the
    trees

The boy that scareth from the spirey wheat
The mellancholy crow—quakes while he weaves
Beneath the ivey tree a hut and seat
Of rustling flags and sedges tyd in sheaves
Or from nigh stubble shocks a shelter thieves
There he doth dithering sit or entertain
His leisure hours down hedges lost to leaves
While spying nests where he spring eggs hath taen
He wishes in his heart twas summer time again

And oft he'll clamber up a sweeing tree
To see the scarlet hunter hurry bye
And feign[1] woud in their merry uproar be
But sullen labour hath its tethering tye
Crows swop around and some on bushes nigh
Watch for a chance when ere he turns away
To settle down their hunger to supply

[1] = fain.

118

From morn to eve his toil demands his stay
Save now and then an hour which leisure steals for
    play

Gaunt greyhounds now their coursing sports impart
Wi long legs stretchd on tip toe for the chase
And short loose ear and eye upon the start
Swift as the wind their motions they unlace
When bobs the hare up from her hiding place
Who in its furry coat of fallow stain
Squats on the lands or wi a dodging pace
Tryes its old coverts of wood grass to gain
And oft by cunning ways makes all their speed in vain

Dull for a time the slumbering weather flings
Its murky prison round then winds wake loud
Wi sudden start the once still forest sings
Winters returning song cloud races cloud
And the orison throws away its shrowd
And sweeps its stretching circle from the eye
Storm upon storm in quick succession crowd
And oer the sameness of the purple skye
Heaven paints its wild irregularity

The shepherd oft foretells by simple ways
The weathers change that will ere long prevail
He marks the dull ass that grows wild and brays
And sees the old cows gad adown the vale
A summer race and snuff the coming gale
The old dame sees her cat wi fears alarm
Play hurly burly races wi its tale

And while she stops her wheel her hands to warm
She rubs her shooting corns and prophecys a storm

Morts are the signs—the stone hid toad will croak
And gobbling turkey cock wi noises vile
Dropping his snout as flaming as a cloak
Loose as a red rag oer his beak the while
Urging the dame to turn her round and smile
To see his uncooth pride her cloaths attack
Sidling wi wings hung down in vapoury broil
And feathers ruffld up while oer his back
His tail spreads like a fan cross wavd wi bars of black

The hog sturts round the stye and champs the straw
And bolts about as if a dog was bye
The steer will cease its gulping cud to chew
And toss his head wi wild and startld eye
At windshook straws—the geese will noise and flye
Like wild ones to the pond—wi matted mane
The cart horse squeals and kicks his partner nigh
While leaning oer his fork the foddering swain
The uproar marks around and dreams of wind and
     rain

And quick it comes among the forest oaks
Wi sobbing ebbs and uproar gathering high
The scard hoarse raven on its cradle croaks
And stock dove flocks in startld terrors flye
While the blue hawk hangs oer them in the skye
The shepherd happy when the day is done
Hastes to his evening fire his cloaths to dry

And forrester crouchd down the storm to shun
Scarce hears amid the strife the poachers muttering
   gun

The ploughman hears the sudden storm begin
And hies for shelter from his naked toil
Buttoning his doublet closer to his chin
He speeds him hasty oer the elting soil
While clouds above him in wild fury boil
And winds drive heavily the beating rain
He turns his back to catch his breath awhile
Then ekes his speed and faces it again
To seek the shepherds hut beside the rushy plain

Oft stripping cottages and barns of thack
Where startld farmer garnerd up his grain
And wheat and bean and oat and barley stack
Leaving them open to the beating rain
The husbandman grieves oer his loss in vain
And sparrows mourn their night nests spoild and bare
The thackers they resume their toils again
And stubbornly the tall red ladders bare
While to oerweight the wind they hang old harrows
   there

Thus wears the month along in checkerd moods
Sunshine and shadow tempest loud and calms
One hour dyes silent oer the sleepy woods
The next wakes loud with unexpected storms
A dreary nakedness the field deforms
Yet many rural sounds and rural sights
Live in the village still about the farms

NOVEMBER

Where toils rude uproar hums from morn till night
Noises in which the ear of industry delights:

Hoarse noise of field-free bull that strides ahead
Of the tail switching herd to feed again
The barking mastiff from his kennel bed
Urging his teazing noise at passing swain
The jostling rumble of the starting wain
From the farm yard where freedoms chance to wait
The turkey drops his snout and geese in vain
Noise at the signal of the opening gate
Then from the clowns whip flyes and finds the chance
    too late

The pigeon wi its breast of many hues
That spangles to the sun turns round and round
About his timid sidling mate and croos
Upon the cottage ridge where oer their heads
The puddock sails oft swopping oer the pen
Where timid chickens from their parent stray
That skulk and scutter neath her wings agen
Nor peeps no more till they have saild away[1]

Such rural sounds the mornings tongue renews
And rural sights swarm on the rustics eye
The billy goat shakes from his beard the dews
And jumps the wall wi country teams to hie
Upon the barn rig at their freedom flye
The spotted guiney fowl—hogs in the stye

[1] Defective stanza.

NOVEMBER

Agen the door in rooting whinings stand
The freed colt drops his head and gallops bye
The boy that holds a scuttle in his hand
Prefering unto toil the commons rushy land

At length the busy noise of toil is still
And industry awhile her care forgoes
When winter comes in earnest to fulfill
Her yearly task at bleak novembers close
And stops the plough and hides the field in snows
When frost locks up the streams in chill delay
And mellows on the hedge the purple sloes
For little birds—then toil hath time for play
And nought but threshers flails awake the dreary day

DECEMBER

CHRISTMASS

Christmass is come and every hearth
Makes room to give him welcome now
Een want will dry its tears in mirth
And crown him wi a holly bough
Tho tramping neath a winters sky
Oer snow track paths and ryhmey[1] stiles
The huswife sets her spining bye
And bids him welcome wi her smiles

[1] = rimy.

124

DECEMBER · CHRISTMASS

Each house is swept the day before
And windows stuck wi evergreens
The snow is beesomd from the door
And comfort crowns the cottage scenes
Gilt holly wi its thorny pricks
And yew and box wi berrys small
These deck the unusd candlesticks
And pictures hanging by the wall

Neighbours resume their anual cheer
Wishing wi smiles and spirits high
Glad christmass and a happy year
To every morning passer bye
Milk maids their christmass journeys go
Accompanyd wi favourd swain
And childern pace the crumping snow
To taste their grannys cake again

Hung wi the ivys veining bough
The ash trees round the cottage farm
Are often stript of branches now
The cotters christmass hearth to warm
He swings and twists his hazel band
And lops them off wi sharpend hook
And oft brings ivy in his hand
To decorate the chimney nook

Old winter whipes his icles bye
And warms his fingers till he smiles
Where cottage hearths are blazing high
And labour resteth from his toils

Wi merry mirth beguiling care
Old customs keeping wi the day
Friends meet their christmass cheer to share
And pass it in a harmless way

Old customs O I love the sound
However simple they may be
What ere wi time has sanction found
Is welcome and is dear to me
Pride grows above simplicity
And spurns it from her haughty mind
And soon the poets song will be
The only refuge they can find

The shepherd now no more afraid
Since custom doth the chance bestow
Starts up to kiss the giggling maid
Beneath the branch of mizzletoe
That neath each cottage beam is seen
Wi pearl-like-berrys shining gay
The shadow still of what hath been
Which fashion yearly fades away

And singers too a merry throng
At early morn wi simple skill
Yet imitate the angels song
And chant their christmass ditty still
And mid the storm that dies and swells
By fits—in humings softly steals
The music of the village bells
Ringing round their merry peals

And when its past a merry crew
Bedeckt in masks and ribbons gay
The 'Morrice danse' their sports renew
And act their winter evening play
The clown-turnd-kings for penny praise
Storm wi the actors strut and swell
And harlequin a laugh to raise
Wears his hump back and tinkling bell

And oft for pence and spicy ale
Wi winter nosgays pind before
The wassail singer tells her tale
And drawls her christmass carrols oer
The prentice boy wi ruddy face
And ryhme[1] bepowderd dancing locks
From door to door wi happy pace
Runs round to claim his 'christmass box'

The block behind the fire is put
To sanction customs old desires
And many a faggots bands are cut
For the old farmers christmass fires
Where loud tongd gladness joins the throng
And winter meets the warmth of may
Feeling by times the heat too strong
And rubs his shins and draws away

While snows the window panes bedim
The fire curls up a sunny charm
Where creaming oer the pitchers rim
The flowering ale is set to warm

---

[1] = rime.

Mirth full of joy as summer bees
Sits there its pleasures to impart
While childern tween their parents knees
Sing scraps of carrols oer by heart

And some to view the winter weathers
Climb up the window seat wi glee
Likening the snow to falling feathers
In fancys infant extacy
Laughing wi superstitious love
Oer visions wild that youth supplyes
Of people pulling geese above
And keeping christmass in the skyes

As tho the homstead trees were drest
In lieu of snow wi dancing leaves
As tho the sundryd martins nest
Instead of icles hung the eaves
The childern hail the happy day
As if the snow was april grass
And pleasd as neath the warmth of may
Sport oer the water froze to glass

Thou day of happy sound and mirth
That long wi childish memory stays
How blest around the cottage hearth
I met thee in my boyish days
Harping wi raptures dreaming joys
On presents that thy coming found
The welcome sight of little toys
The christmass gifts of comers round

The wooden horse wi arching head
Drawn upon wheels around the room
The gilded coach of ginger bread
And many colord sugar plumb
Gilt coverd books for pictures sought
Or storys childhood loves to tell
Wi many a urgent promise bought
To get tomorrows lesson well

And many a thing a minutes sport
Left broken on the sanded floor
When we woud leave our play and court
Our parents promises for more
Tho manhood bids such raptures dye
And throws such toys away as vain
Yet memory loves to turn her eye
And talk such pleasures oer again

Around the glowing hearth at night
The harmless laugh and winter tale
Goes round—while parting friends delight
To toast each other oer their ale
The cotter oft wi quiet zeal
Will musing oer his bible lean
While in the dark the lovers steal
To kiss and toy behind the screen

The yule cake dotted thick wi plumbs
Is on each supper table found
And cats look up for falling crumbs
Which greedy childern litter round

And huswifes sage stuffd seasond chine
Long hung in chimney nook to drye
And boiling eldern berry wine
To drink the christmass eves 'good bye'

JULY (SECOND VERSION)

July the month of summers prime
Again resumes her busy time
Scythes tinkle in each grassy dell
Where solitude was wont to dwell
And meadows they are mad with noise
Of laughing maids and shouting boys
Making up the withering hay
With merry hearts as light as play
The very insects on the ground
So nimbly bustle all around
Among the grass or dusty soil
They seem partakers in the toil
The very landscape reels with life
While mid the busy stir and strife
Of industry the shepherd still
Enjoys his summer dreams at will
Bent oer his hook or listless laid
Beneath the pastures willow shade
Whose foliage shines so cool and grey
Amid the sultry hues of day
As if the mornings misty veil
Yet lingered in their shadows pale
Or lolling in a musing mood
On mounds where saxon castles stood
Upon whose deeply buried walls
The ivyed oaks dark shadow falls
Oft picking up with wondering gaze
Some little thing of other days

JULY (SECOND VERSION)

Saved from the wreck of time—as beads
Or broken pots among the weeds
Of curious shapes—and many a stone
Of roman pavements thickly sown
Oft hoping as he searches round
That buried riches may be found
Tho search as often as he will
His hopes are dissapointed still
And marking oft upon his seat
The insect world beneath his feet
In busy motion here and there
Like visitors to feast or fair
Some climbing up the rushes stem
Hugh steeples height or more to them
With speed that sees no fear to drop
Till perched upon its spirey top
Where they awhile the view survey
Then prune their wings and flit away
Others journying too and fro
Among the grassy woods below
Musing as if they felt and knew
The pleasant scenes they wandered thro
Where each bent round them seems to be
Hugh as a jiant timber tree
While pismires from their castles come
In crowds to seek the litterd crumb
Which he on purpose drops that they
May hawl the heavy loads away
Shaping the while their dark employs
To his own visionary joys
Picturing such a life as theirs
As free from summers sweating cares

JULY (SECOND VERSION)

And inly wishing that his own
Coud meet with joys so thickly sown
Sport seems the all that they pursue
And play the only work they do
The cowboy still cuts short the day
In mingling mischief with his play
Oft in the pond with weeds oer grown
Hurling quick the plashing stone
To cheat his dog who watching lies
And instant plunges for the prize
And tho each effort proves as vain
He shakes his coat and dives again
Till wearied with the fruitless play
Then drops his tail and sneaks away
Nor longer heeds the bawling boy
Who seeks new sports with added joy
And on some banks oer hanging brow
Beats the whasps nest with a bough
Till armys from the hole appear
And threaten vengance in his ear
With such determined hue and cry
As makes the bold besieger flye
Elsewhere fresh mischief to renew
And still his teazing sports pursue
Pelting with excessive glee
The squirrel on the wood land tree
Who nimbles round from grain to grain
And cocks his tail and peeps again
Half pleased as if he thought the fray
Which mischief made was meant for play
Till scared and startled into flight
He instant hurries out of sight
Thus he his leisure hour employs
And feeds on busy meddling joys

JULY (SECOND VERSION)

While in the willow shaded pool
His cattle stand their hides to cool

Loud is the summers busy song
The smalles[t] breeze can find a tongue
Where insects of each tiney size
Grow teazing with their melodys
Till noon burns with its blistering breath
Around and day dyes still as death
The busy noise of man and brute
Is on a sudden lost and mute
The cuckoo singing as she flies
No more to mocking boy replys
Even the brook that leaps along
Seems weary of its bubbling song
And so soft its waters creep
Tired silence sinks in sounder sleep
The cricket on its banks is dumb
The very flies forget to hum
And save the waggon rocking round
The lanscape sleeps without a sound
The breeze is stopt the lazy bough
Hath not a leaf that dances now
The totter grass upon the hill
And spiders threads are standing still
The feathers dropt from more hens wing
Which to the waters surface cling
Are stedfast and as heavy seem
As stones beneath them in the stream
Hawkweeds and Groundsells fanning downs
Unruffled keep their seedy crowns
And in the oven heated air
Not one light thing is floating there

JULY (SECOND VERSION)

—Save that to the earnest eye
The restless heat seems twittering bye
Noon swoons beneath the heat it made
And flowers een wither in the shade
Untill the sun slopes in the west
Like weary traveler glad to rest
On pillard[1] clouds of many hues
Then natures voice its joy renews
And checkerd field and grassy plain
Hum with their summer songs again
A requiem to the days decline
Whose setting sun beams cooly shine
A welcome to days feeble powers
As evening dews on thirsty flowers

Now to the pleasant pasture dells
Where hay from closes sweetly smells
Adown the pathways narrow lane
The milking maiden hies again
With scraps of ballads never dumb
And rosey cheeks of happy bloom
Tanned brown by summers rude embrace
That adds new beautys to her face
And red lips never paled with sighs
And flowing hair and laughing eyes
That oer full many a heart prevailed
And swelling bosom loosly veiled
White as the love it harbours there
Unsullied with the taints of care
The mower gives his labour oer
And on his bench beside the door

[1] = pillowed.

135

JULY (SECOND VERSION)

Sits down to see his childern play
Or smokes his leisure hour away
While from her cage the blackbird sings
That on the wood bine arbour hings
And all with happy joys recieve
The quiet of a summers eve

GLOSSARY

a, on the.
ach, ache.
ant, ain't.

baffles, leggings.
beaver, felt hat resembling fur.
beavering time, time for a break for refreshment.
beetle, heavy mallet used for driving wedges.
bent, coarse grass.
benty, like *bent*.
bleb, see *horse bleb*.
bottle-brush, popular name of horse-tail, mare's tail.
brashy, delicate.
brig, bridge.
bumbarrel, long-tailed tit.
burring, droning, purring.

cag, a small cask, keg.
carless, careless.
carlock, charlock? (could be: (*a*) wild turnip, (*b*) white mustard, or (*c*) charlock).
chimble, to nibble.
clown, yokel, rustic, labourer.
coat, cote.
colter, coulter.
coying, decoying, misleading.
crank, to sing dolefully; to make a harsh noise (Wright cites this example and gives the first meaning).
crick, to bounce under the leg?
crimple, to ruffle; to wrinkle.
crimpling, hobbling.
crimpt, wrinkled.

crizzle, to roughen, as water, when it begins to freeze.
croodle, to huddle, for warmth or protection.
crow pot stones, fossil shells, gryphites.
crump, to crunch.
cucking balls, balls of flowers for throwing in May games.
curnel, kernel.
custom, customary.

dengle, var. of *dangle*.
douse, to drench, soak.
drabble, to draggle, smear, muddy.

edding, a headland, or grass at the end of a field where the plough turns.
eke, to add to, to enlarge.
elting- moulds, the soft ridges of freshly ploughed land. Clare's word *elting* is adapted from this.

feign, fain.
flirt, to flit or flutter.
flittering, fluttering.
flurt, var. of *flirt*.
footbrig, footbridge.
fore, bank, edge or brink of pool?
fore horse, leading horse of a plough team.
frail, flail.
fret, to thaw.
frumity, frumenty.

gadding, moving restlessly.

137

gads, gad-flies.
gangling, jangling.
gingling, jingling.
gleg, to look asquint, to peep.
glib, smooth, slippery.
grizzle, to darken, to turn lowering.

hant, to haunt; also *sb.*
higgling, searching. Cf. Anglo-Saxon, *hicgan*, to try, to search thoroughly.
hilo, high-low; a heavy laced boot.
hing, to hang.
hoisd, hoisted.
horsbee, (a) horse bot-fly, or (b) cleg.
horse bleb, marsh marigold.
huddle, hurry in a crouching manner.
hugh, huge.
hulk, a temporary shelter, used by shepherds in the lambing-season.
hurd, to hoard, store.
hurring, hurrying.
hussle, to toss. Cf. 'pitch and hussel'.

ickle, icicle.
icle, icicle.
iron weed, (a) hard-head (*Centaurea nigra*) or (b) viper's bugloss (*Echium vulgare*).

jeniten, early sweet apple.
jilt, to throw underhand with a quick and suddenly arrested motion.
jumping flye, turnip fly.

keck horn, a 'horn' made from the dried stalk of the hemlock, cow parsley, or any other umbelliferous plant.
knap, to bite, crop.
knat, gnat.

land, an arable division of a furlong in an open field.
lare, resting-place; the place animals are accustomed to stay in; a clearing.
leam, husk.
lob, to walk heavily.
loose, to lose.
lushing, abundant, luxurious.

mawl, to drag along wearily.
midgeon, dim. of *midge*.
moiling, working hard, toiling.
moment, momentary.
morts, many, lots.
mozzle, mottled? mossed over?

nauntle, to hold oneself erect.

oddling, odd.
oggle, cuddle; var. of *huggle*?

pales, palings.
pansion, a large earthenware bowl.
pillard, pillowed.
pismire, ant.
platt, a flat stretch of ground?
poddle, to toddle.
pooty, a snail-shell, esp. of *Helix nemoralis*.
princifeather, lilac.
pudgy, watery, full of puddles.

rail, the landrail, the corncrake.
ramping, romping, eager, wild.
rid, rode, pret. of *ride*.

rig, ridge.
rock, to sway, to walk unsteadily.
rott, rat.
ruffs, a variety of gooseberry. Yellow Rough was a nineteenth-century variety listed by Hogg in 1850.
ryhme, rime.

sawn, saunter.
scratt, scratch.
scutter, to scuttle, or to run briskly.
scuttle, basket, nose-bag?
sheeptray, a large hurdle.
shill, shrill.
shoy, shy.
sifter, kitchen shovel, fire shovel.
sile, to glide, fleet past.
slive, to slide, to slip past quickly.
snuff, to sniff.
snuft, to sniff.
soodle, to dawdle, saunter.
sputter, to splutter.
starnel, starling.
stint, to trouble, vex? Perhaps in the sense of limiting the area of grass on which the horse feeds, by frightening him back.
streak, to stretch.
(on the) *strunt*, strut.

struttle, minnow or stickleback.
stulp, the stump of a tree.
stunt, steep; sharp.
sturnel, starling.
sturt, to startle, disturb.
sue, to sew.
sutty, sooty.
swaily, shady, cool.
swathy, swarthy?
swee, to sway.
swive, OE. swifan to move in a course, sweep: ME. to copulate. Seems to have the meaning 'to bunch'.
swop, to pounce, as a bird on its prey.

ted, to turn new-mown hay.
thack, thatch.
throngd, busy, occupied.
totter grass, quaking grass, *Briza media*.
toze, to pluck, to snatch.
tray, hurdle. See also *sheeptray*.
truck, to tuck?
tuggle, to pull, to handle roughly.
tutle, to tootle.
twitter, to flicker.

waffle, to yap, to bark.
while, until.

younker, youngster.

OXFORD

MORE OXFORD PAPERBACKS

Details of a selection of other Oxford Paperbacks follow. A complete list of Oxford Paperbacks, including The World's Classics, Twentieth-Century Classics, OPUS, Past Masters, Oxford Authors, Oxford Shakespeare, and Oxford Paperback Reference, is available in the UK from the General Publicity Department, Oxford University Press (RS), Walton Street, Oxford, OX2 6DP.

In the USA, complete lists are available from the Paperbacks Marketing Manager, Oxford University Press, 200 Madison Avenue, New York, NY 10016.

Oxford Paperbacks are available from all good bookshops. In case of difficulty, customers in the UK can order direct from Oxford University Press Bookshop, 116 High Street, Oxford, Freepost, OX1 4BR, enclosing full payment. Please add 10 per cent of the published price for postage and packing.

THE TAIN

Translated by Thomas Kinsella

The Tain is a translation from the *Tàin Bó Cuailnge,* centre-piece of the eighth-century Ulster cycle of heroic tales, and Ireland's nearest approach to a great epic. It tells the story of a giant cattle-raid, the invasion of Ulster by the armies of Medb and Ailill, queen and king of Connacht, and their allies, seeking to carry off the great Brown Bull of Cuailnge.

'This magnificent version of the early epic . . . deserves to be as widely read for its literary significance as it is already widely coveted for its beauty as a book.' *Listener*

'Kinsella has given us something both old and new . . . a most distinguished book.' *Irish Times*

THE RIVERSIDE CHAUCER

Following publication of F. N. Robinson's second edition of *The Works of Geoffrey Chaucer* in 1957, was a dramatic increase in Chaucer scholarship. This has not only enriched our understanding of Chaucer's art, but has also enabled scholars, working for the first time with all source-material, to recreate Chaucer's authentic texts.

For this new edition, the team of experts at the Riverside Institute have completely re-edited all the works, added glossaries to appear alongside text and greatly expanded the introductory material, explanatory notes, textual notes, and bibliography.

In short, *The Riverside Chaucer* is the fruit of many years' study—the most authentic and exciting edition available of Chaucer's Complete Works.

TENNYSON
Poems and Plays
Edited by T. Herbert Warren
Revised and enlarged by Frederick Page

This edition of the poetical works of Tennyson includes his juvenilia and, in an appendix, some 45 poems excluded from the poet's own final edition, together with his verse dramas, *Queen Mary, Harold, Becket, The Promise of May, The Foresters,* and the short plays, *The Cup* and *The Falcon.* The arrangement is chronological and the notes reproduced are Tennyson's own.

The edition, first published in the Oxford Standard Authors series, is based on *Poems of Tennyson 1830–1870* edited by Sir T. Herbert Warren and first published in 1912: this was revised and expanded in 1953 by the late Frederick Page, to take in the plays and the poems published up to the author's death in 1892.

COLERIDGE
Poetical Works
Revised by Ernest Hartley Coleridge

This edition by Ernest Hartley Coleridge, grandson of the poet, contains a complete and authoritative text of Coleridge's poems. Here are his earliest extant teenage poems, his masterly meditative pieces, and the extraordinary supernatural poems— 'The Rime of the Ancient Mariner', 'Kubla Khan', and 'Christabel'.

The text follows that of the 1834 edition, the last published in the author's lifetime. The poems are printed, so far as is possible, in chronological order, with Coleridge's own notes as well as textual and bibliographical notes by the editor.

SELECTED POEMS AND PROSE OF JOHN CLARE

Chosen and edited by
Eric Robinson and Geoffrey Summerfield

Illustrated by David Gentleman

This selection by Eric Robinson and Geoffrey Summerfield is based upon their study of Clare's original manuscripts and is an authentic reconstruction of what Clare actually wrote, in some cases going behind printed versions of his work to the primary sources, and in others presenting work never before published. It reveals the variety of Clare's writing, his poetic strengths and sensitivities, and defies the labelling of him as a 'peasant poet' or simple lyricist. Here is to be found also the best of Clare's prose—descriptive and political—which combines the traditions both of Cobbett and White of Selborne.

SPENSER

Poetical Works

Edited by J. C. Smith and E. de Selincourt

In this edition of Spenser's complete Poetical Works, first published in the Oxford Standard Authors series in 1912, the text of the *Faerie Queene* is reproduced from J. C. Smith's Clarendon Press edition of 1909; the text of the *Minor Poems*, save for the correction of a few errors, follows the de Selincourt Oxford English Texts edition of 1910. To the poems have been added the *Correspondence of Spenser and Harvey*, printed from the original editions of 1580, and a valuable Glossary compiled by H. Alexander.

The volume opens with a substantial introduction by E. de Selincourt in which a biographical account is followed by a critical section dealing with, among other topics, plot and allegory, characterization, diction, versification, and style in the *Faerie Queene*.

BYRON

Poetical Works

Edited by Frederick Page

New edition corrected by John Jump

Lord Byron, in many ways the archetype of the Romantic era and a poet whose moods swing between the cynical and the transcendental, has delighted subsequent generations with his poetry as he delighted and scandalized his own.

The text of this edition by Frederick Page, containing nearly all of Byron's published poems together with the poet's own notes, has been revised by John Jump. First published in The Oxford Poets in 1896, it was included in the Oxford Standard Authors series in 1904, and many times reprinted.

METAPHYSICAL LYRICS AND POEMS OF THE SEVENTEENTH CENTURY

Edited by H. J. C. Grierson

This classic anthology, first published in 1921, has been instrumental in reviving interest in the seventeenth-century metaphysical poets and in securing for them the high reputation they now enjoy. Included in this representative selection are love poems, divine poems, elegies, satires, epistles, and meditations by over twenty-five poets. The poems range from Suckling's impish love songs to Donne's holy sonnets, from Marvell's 'The Garden' to George Herbert's 'Easter Wings'. They exemplify the intellectual wit, the learned imagery, the ability to articulate experience, and above all the peculiar blend of passion and thought which characterize metaphysical poetry.

The brilliant essay by Sir Herbert Grierson, who made this selection, serves as an illuminating introduction to this group of poets, and has become a classic piece of criticism.